MW01526465

ACKNOWLEDGEMENTS

I want to personally thank Kacey for allowing me to grow and to heal our friendship. I also would like to thank Mr. Darnell Carter for running a not so conventional anger management class, I am dedicated to change and this man showed me some ways to do that. I also would like to thank God for my mother, father, and grandparents. Even through their struggles they raised a man who wants change in the world. I would also like to thank my brothers Damon Kirks and Rick Wilcox for always being there to protect me and make me realize that I was an ass hole when I was in denial about being one. Thank you Angela Welch for drying my tears and for kisses on the cheek. I also want to thank Sonja Wilson for always speaking positively, and for being a great friend. My siblings Aaron Harris, Rasheedah Irby, Aneesah Bowie, Kareem Ali, Sakinah Bryant, and my main man, my baby brother and best friend Jamal Manning. You have been riding with your big bro since he has become a grown man. Last but not least my wife Crissie Jordan-Ali may she rest in peace for loving me in spite of all my indiscretions, and giving me two wonderful children and the best step son a man could ask for, all while you were dealing with mental illness. Love is the best emotion in the world and God is love!

I would like to thank God for giving this vision to Muhammad, and for Muhammad's patience with me. I want to thank my son for his continual inspiration, I do what I do to glorify God and be a good example to my son. I want to thank my parents for their unconditional love and support. I want to thank all the people who counseled me through my issues that came as a result of my life struggles. And lastly, I thank God for allowing situations in my life that were so painful to be used to help others! God you are my hero!!!!!

If you or anyone you know is involved in a domestic/intimate partner violence relationship you can contact The Domestic Violence Hotline at 1-800-799-7233 or www.thehotline.org

Muhammad and Kacey can be reached on Facebook HIS SIDE HER SIDE, or at hshsbook@gmail.com.

Table of Contents

HER SIDE

Introduction

The first book I wrote is titled, "Deliverance from Sexual Sin", and it's all about how God delivered me from a life of sexual promiscuity to now over 10 years of abstinence. Not only was I extremely promiscuous, but I also found myself drawn to the same type of men, men who were controlling, possessive, and abusive. In my first book, I talked about an abusive relationship I was in with a man named, "Muslim". He is the co-author of this book. All I can say is this book is only in your hands because God is the only one who can turn a mess into a message.

It is my prayer that every male and female who has ever been in, or is currently in an abusive relationship, will get something out of this book that will cause them to form a relationship with God, receive counseling, and make the decision to only engage in healthy relationships. No matter if you are the victim or the abuser, you deserve healthy relationships.

I would love for males and females to glean something from his side and my side of our story. Please enjoy what we have labored over in order for it to be a blessing to you! Share this book with everyone you know! And thank you so much for supporting us!

Chapter 1: About Me

If you haven't read my first book Deliverance from Sexual Sin, this will be new for you, but if you have much of this will be familiar. I am so thankful you will be able to hear from Muhammad, because you will get his view point, and his perspective.

I grew up in a two parent household, with an older brother, and a dog, in the suburbs. Our suburb was unique, in that it was predominately black and middle class. About a year ago, I had a memory come back to me that lay hidden in my brain for over 30 years. It wasn't in my first book because it had already been published. Between the ages of 3&4 I was molested. I have no idea who the perpetrator was but I know it was a male. I am currently pursuing my Master's in Clinical Mental Health Counseling, and it wasn't until I took a class last semester called, "Counseling Survivors of Childhood Sexual Abuse", that I realized our brain has a way of protecting us from some trauma's we experience by not allowing us to remember them. I truly believe God's grace kept that memory hidden until I could handle it and understand it.

One of the books I had to read for that class was titled, "The Body Remembers", by Babette Rothschild. This book educated me on how my mind

7

didn't allow me to remember, but my physical body displayed the effects of the molestation. Two long term effects that are still a part of me today as a result of the sexual abuse are anxiety and fear. I truly believe the male who did this was someone I did not know. I may never know who he was, but my focus is on continuing to get the healing I need, in order to manage the anxiety I struggle with.

Fast forward to age 13, and I was raped by someone I knew very well, and had known for 4 years. He was two years older than me and someone I trusted very much. I was an innocent 13 year old, who was sheltered by her parents, and didn't even know what sex was. He was the first boy I ever kissed and he had to teach me how to do that. I remember everything about the day he raped me, even down to the moment I was lying on my back looking up at the sky to escape the pain of him forcing himself inside of me. He convinced me afterwards that I wanted it because I allowed him to French kiss me. And since I was a very naïve 13 year old, I believed him for many years. Yes, for many years believed if you kiss a boy then that means you want to have sex with him.

When I was 17, I was with a guy I really liked and I made him wait before I had sex with him. He took me to his homecoming dance and I decided that would be the night. I was so happy to give myself to him, and it turned out to be a wonderful night in that motel room. The next day he told me he had been seeing someone else for the past month, and the only reason he was still with me was because he wanted to have sex with me first. He said there was no way he would walk away from me after he had been waiting months to get in my pants. Now that he had gotten in my pants, he could walk away and enjoy his new relationship. I was devastated so devastated, and somehow this triggered me to realize the sex I thought I had at 13 was truly rape. It felt like I was being raped all over again because he used me just for sex. My first 3 experiences in my life with sex were all negative, what did I do to deserve this?????

So from the age of 17-32 I went on a sex spree that was triggered by the realization of the rape. Yes, for many years I had sex with many men out of fear that I would be raped again, and the remainder of those years I chose to have sex with limitless amounts of men because I was convinced that all guys really wanted me for was sex anyway, I mean what else did I have to offer them?

So now you are probably wondering, "Why in the heck is she talking about sexual abuse and promiscuity in a book about domestic violence"? I am one of many women and men who are survivors of domestic violence and I am sure if you got all of us in one room we could relate to each other's childhood into adulthood, but none of our stories would be the exact same, but some would be similar. I want you to have an understanding of the things that happened in my life that led me to believe I was the ugliest most worthless female on this earth. And why I believed I deserved every slap, punch, and near death experience from the men who abused me. So my sexual abuse and promiscuity is very relevant to my history of domestic violence. My co-author was the last man to physically abuse me. There were others before him and after him who verbally and emotionally abused me. I want to talk about the guys before Muhammad so you can get a glimpse of the progression.

I was 19 when I experienced domestic violence for the first time. Some memories are vague, some are clear, and even in my 40's, some memories are just now coming to me. He was the first guy to put his hands on me and the first guy who was actually attractive. Why does a nice looking, popular guy want anything to do with a "nobody" like me. So I immediately had sex with him in order to keep him. He never forced himself on me sexually, but he was sexually aggressive, if that makes sense. He was physically aggressive on two separate occasions, the first time he got angry with me and slapped me and pushed my head into a kitchen cabinet. The second time he wanted me to engage in a sexual act, and I guess I wasn't doing it fast enough for him and he slapped me. On both occasions I can remember responding to him by immediately obeying whatever he wanted and it never entered my mind to fight back or run. At the age of 19 I was convinced that I needed to be a man's sex slave and punching bag.

He lived in Cleveland and I was in school in Atlanta, and we met on one of my visits home for winter break. He was extremely controlling and he didn't trust me at all. This meant I had to always let him know where I was and if I wasn't home by a certain time, there was always a problem. I would have to call him when I got home so he would know I was there, and if I would call him too late he would verbally abuse me. Thank goodness we didn't live together, because I am sure there would have been physical consequences for that. The lack of trust escalated when I went back to Atlanta for school. You truly have to be a victim of domestic violence to understand the power your abuser has over you, even hundreds of miles away. I still had to check in with him all the way from Atlanta, and the same fear I had of him while in Cleveland was the same fear I had when I went back to Atlanta.

One night I was in my dorm room waiting on him to call me. If I wasn't in my dorm room at night when he would call me, he automatically thought I was cheating on him. And in my mind I felt I needed to overly assure him I was not cheating on him, so I would comply with all his wishes. One night one of the fraternities was crossing a new line of pledges and I could hear them outside of my dorm room. Do I stay in my room or do I go see the show? Maybe he won't call, and I will just go and watch the line march up to the yard and not stay for the entire show. When I realized one of my friends was on the line I had to stay and watch the whole show. As soon as it was over and I congratulated him, I sprinted back to my dorm room, hoping he didn't call while I was gone. As I rushed off the elevator

I could hear my phone ringing all the way down the hall, and my rush turned into a freeze. My heart started pounding so fast, and I began walking slowly to my room hoping the phone would stop ringing, because I knew what was going to happen when I answered, and it would be my fault. The phone stops ringing, but of course I did not feel relieved, because I knew I would still have to call him. Why did that fraternity have to cross a line tonight? Why did I disobey him and not stay in my room and wait for his call? Why do I continue to give him a reason not to trust me? Now I will be the reason he has to be stressed out and angry. Now I will be the reason he won't trust me and I will have to start all over again in earning his trust. The phone starts ringing again and I know I can't avoid it this time or there will really be great consequences. Will he believe me when I tell him I was just watching the fraternity cross? Wait a minute, I can't tell him that because he will think I was messing around with one of the pledges. Well he is going to accuse me anyway, so I might as well tell the truth. "Kacey, answer the phone because you need to bring him some security." "Hello". "Where the he_ _ have you been you stupid Bi_ _ _?" I never got a chance to explain because he spent the whole time accusing me of being with another man and cussing me out. He let me know I was in for the beating of my life whenever I came home for the summer. He told me I better answer every call from then on or he would come down and make me pay. Well, I did make sure I was in my dorm room on the days and times he told me to, it was like I had a curfew. When it was time to go home for the summer, I got up the courage to not call him and let him know. He called and called until he got tired of me not responding. I am so glad I was able to let go, because he really scared me and I truly didn't know if he would be able to stop beating me once he got started.

I can remember being a kid overhearing conversations from some adults about a husband who was beating his wife all the time and I can remember saying I would never find myself in that situation. As I stated in my first book, most abusers don't begin the relationship abusing. They are very good at what they do and they know which person is a prime candidate to be victimized. They will make you believe that you are the most desirable person they have ever met, and that turns into you spending as much time with them as they want to spend with you. They get you to believe all you need is them, which causes you to believe you are the best thing that ever happened to them. They get you to believe that they know what is best for you even better than you know, so when they tell you that you don't need your friends or family anymore you believe it. They get you to believe they can't exist without you, so then you believe they are the only man in the world who truly wants you. Then they get you to believe you would be nothing without them, so you become dependent on them for everything, including how you should dress.

They get you to believe if you leave no one else will want you, so you stay and endure all the pain because you don't want to be alone. They get you to believe that it's not abuse because they didn't hit you with a fist, so when you hear about abusive relationships you don't look at yours as one. They get you to believe it was your fault they hit you and if you would just "act right" they will never have to hit you, so you try your hardest never to repeat the same negative behavior. And when they tell you they will kill you if you leave, you believe them because you have believed everything else they have said and done.........

At the end of this book there will still be some of you who will say victims of domestic violence are dumb and stupid. It is my prayer that most of you will empathize with victims and not become another abuser in their life by verbally putting them down for being in an abusive relationship. No one wakes up as a kid and says, "I want to find a person who will verbally and physically abuse me when I grow up". Or "I think I will spend my life beating every person I'm in a relationship with when I grow up". I am not excusing these behaviors I just truly believe if a person knows better in their head and their heart, they will do better.

A couple of years after I ended this relationship, I met a guy who was friends with some of my friends. Many of us would hang out a lot on campus and drink and get high. He had a girlfriend and I knew her as well, but she didn't hang out with us. He was someone I could easily talk to, and after the death of my grandfather he reached out to me for support. He was there for me and I truly appreciated it because it was just what I needed. One day we were hanging out at my place getting high and the next thing I knew we were having sex. It wasn't my intention to cross the line, but once I did, I didn't feel bad about it. I didn't even feel guilty when I would see his girlfriend on campus. Then she got pregnant, and the two of them got engaged and moved in together, and this all happened while I was at home for the summer. He was calling me through the whole summer telling me how much he missed me and how he couldn't wait for me to get back. We were having lots of sex before I went home for the summer, so I was telling him the same thing, however part of me started feeling guilty. When I would get off the phone with him I would think to myself, "I can't continue to see him and he has a baby on the way." So I made the decision to end the affair when I got back to Atlanta.

The first day I got back to Atlanta I called him because I wanted to quickly end it so I could move on. But when I saw his face, all that went out of the window and we were in the bed. We continued for a couple months and as her stomach got bigger, the guilt began to consume me again. So I decided homecoming weekend I would break it off. He came over to get high with me and some of our friends. I decided to have some goodbye sex first and then tell him it was over. The next morning before he left I told him I was ending it with him because I wanted to respect his relationship. I saw a look in his eyes I had never seen before. He told me he would kill me before he allowed me to leave him, and the next thing I knew he became very physical with me. He began biting my legs really hard and as I hit his head to stop him, he would bite even harder. At that moment I stopped hitting him because he was biting me like a savage animal. When he was done I had at least six huge bite marks on both of my legs. I am not a light-skinned female and each bruise was extremely dark with very visible bite marks all around them. Before he left he made sure I knew he was a permanent part of my life regardless of what I said.

As he left out of my home, I sat on my bedroom floor frozen. There were so many thoughts flowing in my mind. Did that just happen? He has never acted like this before, and why would he do this, I'm just his side chick? Who abuses the side chick just because she wants to leave? He must really have some serious feelings for me, feelings that go beyond good sex, these are REAL feelings.

As I tried to lift one of my legs, I felt the most intense pain ever. It took a while for me to finally get off the floor and into my bed, and I stayed there for a long time. I lived off campus so I missed a couple of days of school, because it was hard for me to walk around the house, so there was no way I could walk to school. He called and called and I let him talk to my answering machine. The first couple of messages were messages of apologies and then the nice messages turned into threats because I continued to avoid him. One day he showed up at my house. Seeing his face and hearing him plead with me to open the door, caused me to let my guard down and let him come in. He told me that he just couldn't bear to be without me and that's the only reason he abused me because he was scared of losing me. I asked him why he would go to that extreme when he already has someone and he said it was because I was special, and what we had was special. I told him I wasn't changing my mind and he became enraged and began punching me where the bite marks were and reminded me he would kill me if I didn't change my mind.

After that day I conceded and accepted my victim role. He must truly love me, otherwise he would just walk away and live happily ever after with his fiancé and baby. He remained in my life and he came and went as he pleased having sex with me and beating me whenever the mood hit him. He would beat me for no reason, and I truly believe he did it because he knew he could. Or maybe I was his stress reliever, or maybe it was so I would never get the idea to break things off with him.

He was pledging a fraternity and he and some of his line brothers needed to use my refrigerator to store some food. They brought the food and I put it all away as they stood in the kitchen talking, I felt like I was the one on line. When his line brothers left, he pushed me in the bedroom and wanted to know why I was bending over in the kitchen with my butt in the air in front of his line brothers. He said I was doing it on purpose because I wanted them to look at my butt. I told him I wasn't doing it on purpose, I always bend over like that. He showed me the proper way to bend over and told me that's how I better bend over when I'm around other men. After he told me this he beat me up because he said I disrespected and embarrassed him in front of his line brothers. He told me if I ever cheat on him it's going to end bad for me. I apologized and promised him I would never bend over in front of another man or cheat on him. I literally would not talk to other guys who tried to talk to me and I would not let him see me talking to other guys on campus unless he knew them, because I didn't want him thinking I was being unfaithful. At this point, I believed he loved me more than he loved his fiancé. When I would see her on campus I would feel sorry for her, imagine that I felt sorry for her. Why did I feel sorry for her? Because now he wants me all to himself and he doesn't want me with another man, I must be special!!!!!!!

Every time he called to come over I had to say yes, because it meant he wanted sex and I better not deny him. She was close to having the baby so she was not having sex with him, so I definitely had to fill that void. One night he came over and there was something so different about him. He had a look in his eyes I had never seen before. He wasn't there 5 minutes before he lit into me. He beat me and beat me in ways he never had before. Usually he would bite, punch, or slap, but this night he was on a rampage doing all of that and more. He was on top of me choking me so hard I was literally seeing little flashes of light. Then he told me he wanted to have sex, but I was so tired and in so much pain from the beating I told him no and asked him if I could please rest first. He became more enraged and pulled my clothes off and began grabbing my pubic hair, trying to pull it out, and he was also biting me in my vaginal area. I begged him to please stop because I was in so much pain but he wouldn't stop. Then he forced himself inside of me at the same time I was begging him to please not make me have sex with him. He wouldn't stop and with every stroke, he punched me in the face until I became quiet. As much as I didn't want to have sex with him, he was being too violent and I couldn't fight him any longer. I let him continue to have his way with me sexually until he was satisfied. After he finished raping me, he continued beating me. I don't know where he was getting all this energy from, it was after midnight when he came over and it had been hours later at this point. He put a belt around my neck and dragged me around my bedroom floor and made me act like a dog. He made me bow down to him and make dog sounds. He made it known that he was my master and I was under his control. He literally abused me until sunrise and he finally fell asleep from exhaustion, and I was finally able to get a break. I was so exhausted because this went on for at least 6 hours. I was so scared to go to sleep because I didn't want him to wake up first and catch me off guard. I couldn't stop replaying in mind what happened, and as I watched him sleep I asked myself, "What did I do that made him beat me this severely"? When he woke up he told me to fix him breakfast. I made him a nice breakfast and he was quiet the whole time he ate, and I remained quiet as well. I didn't want to say or do anything that would send him back into the rampage I just endured all night long. After he finished eating he told me he wanted to have sex and I immediately gave in. He made love to me in such a romantic way, which caused me to forgive him for all that abuse he inflicted on me. He even kissed all of my bruises and apologized as he kissed them. Once we finished making love I wanted to lay in his arms all day, but he said he had to go home, and I knew I had to let him go. I later found out he had used cocaine right before he came over and that's why he was so energized and so abusive. God was truly watching over me that night because I don't know how I lived through that.

The abuse continued for a couple more months and I finally realized if I don't get out of this I may not make it out alive. I finally got some strength and began avoiding his calls and avoiding him on campus. One day as I was walking home from school, and he drove up from behind me and I managed to get in the house before he made it to the door. The next day I was coming out of class and he cornered me, put this arm against my throat, and told me I better stop avoiding him or I would regret it. Something had to be done, this was my last semester and I was failing some classes because of avoiding him and the stress. I called one of my ex's because I didn't know who else to turn to. He picked me up and I told him everything, and when we got to his house he told me he would take care of him. My ex was one of those guys who had spent time and jail and had no problem going back. I told him he wasn't worth him going to jail, but I asked him if I could use his car because I couldn't miss another class and I didn't want him driving up on me as I walked to and from school.

He agreed to let me use his car for a week and then I needed to make a decision, or he was going to do something to him. When he and I were together I remembered how he kept his gun on him at all times so I knew I needed to make a decision within that week. That night he let me stay at his house, held me, kissed me and left me to get some rest. In that moment I wanted so badly for him to have sex with me, but I now appreciate the fact that he didn't take advantage of me in that vulnerable state. He still holds a special place in my heart for making my safety a priority for him. When the week was up, I went to the campus police to file a report. A female campus officer took my statement, took pictures of the faint bite marks on my legs, and forwarded the information to the police. The officer was kind enough to give me rides to and from school. I finally got the phone call that he had been arrested. The next day I went to his hearing and his fiancé and baby were there. I felt so ashamed and nervous, but I had to pursue this. He made bail and I was scared because I didn't know if he would retaliate.

The rumors were swirling all around campus and I was the villain. He and his fiancé were telling everyone that I liked rough sex and I was lying about the abuse. I was labeled as crazy and a hoe. I felt like I was being abused all over again, and my circle of friends was now smaller.

Most of our mutual friends decided to support him. However, one of them told me in secret that he believed my side of the story because he had been abusing his fiancé for years. At this point I am so angry because I wanted to know how could she support him and believe him, when he was abusing her too. I now know I had no right to be mad at her, because she was a victim just like me and just because I got the courage to file charges it didn't mean she had the courage. She had more to lose and who would take care of her and the baby?

I grew up in church, but I ran far away from church when I got to college. One day I was really having a bad day because of all the indirect abuse I was experiencing and I went to talk to a faculty member who was in my corner. He wasn't in his office, but his secretary told me she wanted to talk to me. She said that morning in her prayer time the Lord showed her my face and told her things about me that only God could have told her. It was that day that I realized God was real and I wanted to know Him. As I walked home from school that day I told God I didn't want to live like that anymore. It was in that moment that I realized the alcohol and marijuana really clouded my judgement and I needed to stop. I asked God to help me and he immediately took the desire for alcohol and marijuana away from me. When the semester was over I came home and decided to finish my degree here. Two years later I got a phone call from the Prosecutor in Atlanta asking me if I still wanted to pursue the charges against him. Seriously? I had moved on with my life and forgiven him so I told them to drop the case. Little did I know, I was walking into a very similar situation......

Chapter 2: Our Relationship

I would like to begin this chapter by saying if you read my first book you may notice some deletions or additions to our story. It has nothing to do with any fabrications and everything to do with some memories now being clearer to me. Muhammad remembers so much more than I do about our relationship and it has truly helped me a lot. This past weekend Muhammad and I met and it was a great meeting. We discussed what we were going to include in the book. As we were talking I just had to ask him what it was like to be in a relationship with me. Yes, I had a lot to say about him in my first book and I will have a lot to say about him in this book. But I wanted to know about me, because I know I can be a handful. And it was good to know that some of the weaknesses I identified in myself were the same weaknesses Muhammad said contributed to our unhealthy relationship.

Here is our story! I was coming out of a very unhealthy relationship with an older, married man, who was a supervisor at my job, when I met Muhammad. Yes, I needed you to know that I willingly carried on a relationship with a married man, so you would know my choices in men were not the best. Now back to Muhammad. We met at our place of employment, I had been there for about a year and he was a new employee. I was quickly drawn to him, and for some reason he was drawn to me.

We began seeing each other and surprisingly for some reason, we did not sleep together quick. I thought we had, but Muhammad reminded me that we had not slept together quick. We actually went on dates, and yes I had been on dates before, but it wasn't often and I rarely went on more than one date with a man. Muhammad had two daughters when we met. He was not the first guy I dated with kids, however he was the first guy I dated who had his kids often, and one of them lived with him. She was a very cute little girl, but at the time I was 24, with no children of my own and it was a major adjustment for me.

I have to side bar really quickly. In my experience, it appears that some single parents automatically assume the person they are dating is a "parent figure" or wants to be involved with their kids. I was a woman without kids, who had no knowledge of what it is like to be a mother, or a mother figure, and I'm 24 years old, fresh out of the club and drug lifestyle. It's all about me, and even though I like you and want to be with you, I have no concept of the reality that I have to accept your children as well. I said all that to say, it is important for all of us as single parents to make sure the person we are dating knows we have kids up front. We don't have to introduce our kids to them too soon, but the reality is, some people don't want to date people who have children, and they have that right, and we as single parents can't be offended by that. There are even some single parents who don't want to date people who have kids, and that is their right as well! And those who don't have children be honest with yourself about whether you want to date someone with children. And please be honest with that person, because if they are good parents, their kids will be around. Okay, I went down that path for this reason. Internally, I struggled greatly being in a relationship with Muhammad, due to him having a child full time and one that would be around occasionally. I don't know if Muhammad ever picked up on the fact that I struggled, but it contributed to some of my negativity within our relationship. And it wasn't that I didn't like his children, because I did. It was because I was already struggling being responsible for my own emotions, and adding kids to that was overwhelming.

Now back to me and Muhammad. I fell hard for him quickly as I stated, and one of the reasons is because I fell for every guy quickly and another reason was I wanted to make the married guy I had just ended things with, jealous. Yes we all worked together and so I wanted the married guy to see that someone else had me. And it definitely worked because the married guy tried to tell me all the reasons I shouldn't be with Muhammad, which made me want to be with Muhammad even more.

I think we officially became a couple about 3 months after we met, he will probably have a more accurate time frame for you. Every conversation we have had recently about this book, made me realize my memory has been greatly impacted by the trauma I have experienced in my life. I do remember the beginning of our relationship being good. Muhammad was very charming and plus I had not had many "boyfriends" at this point in my life. I was used to most guys just wanting me for sex. I definitely wasn't the girl you wanted to introduce to anybody in your family, and definitely not your mother. Keep all of this in mind, because I am not exactly like every other person who has been abused, but I want you to understand why I stayed in this relationship for so long. When you have rarely been the main chick, and a guy like Muhammad is giving you so much attention, taking you out in public, and not just using you for a booty call, you want to hold on to a guy like that no matter how tough times get. But I now look back and realize the real reason I wanted to hold on to him was because of the familiarity.

Before my relationship with Muhammad I had been involved with a couple of married men, an engaged man, and any other man that wanted me. Prior to Muhammad I had a spiritual awakening. I decided I wanted to know God for myself, so I stopped smoking, drinking, and doing drugs. I was back in church on a weekly basis, and I wanted to do the right thing for a change. Now that I look back on it, Muhammad was like my "New Beginning". I chose to be a girlfriend, and not a side chick. I chose to be faithful to one guy and not deal with multiple guys at a time. This would be good for me because I had been through so much in my life. I was making great money at my job, so Muhammad and I did a lot of things together. And I didn't mind spending money on us, because I was just happy to be going on dates, and being seen in public with a guy, versus motel rooms and back seats of cars. Plus we worked together, and everyone there knew I was his woman. I was number 1, not 2, 3, etc.

I will never forget the day he invited me to the neighborhood cookout he and his friends would do annually. We walked hand in hand and he introduced me to all of his friends. Now some of you who have experienced life with low self-esteem, a history of abuse, always being the one who looks average to others, and never being the prettiest girl to anybody, know exactly why, at the age of 24, this was such a big deal to me. I felt like I was somebody, like I was seen by others, like I was important. I don't know if I expressed this to Muhammad back then, but he truly made me feel like a Queen for the day, heck for months. He truly could have gotten anything from me, I was his and nothing else in the world mattered. While at the cookout, I noticed a couple of females, mainly one, giving me this look like she had a real problem with me. I didn't know why, I just knew she made me feel very uncomfortable. Don't forget about her, because I am going to get back to her soon.

At this point in my life I am living with my parents and he is living with his mother and daughter, and we don't have much privacy. So I decided, with a little nudging from him to get my own apartment. This would be my first time, outside of being in college in Atlanta that I would be living on my own, and that's when we began playing house. He was at my apartment so much he may as well have been on the lease, but there were some days he would go back home to fulfill his fatherly duties.

Everything was great, and in my reality, all great things must come to an end. I don't remember how this all blew up, I'm sure Muhammad has the details, but I found out that he and the female,(giving me the evil eye at the cookout), were having some great sex behind my back. Not only did she work with us, but she also lived in the same complex he lived in. So on the nights he wasn't with me playing house, he was with her making porn. I was so hurt, first because my happy "new beginnings" had turned into a nightmare, and also I found out there were people at our job that knew about them, so now I look like a fool at work. I felt as if I was getting payback for all the married and engaged men I had slept with. As much as I wanted to break up with him, I couldn't. I felt I deserved this for all the wrong I had done in my life.

One night, he and I laid in the bed and talked about his infidelity. I wanted to know why and I wanted details (why do we ask for details????) I laid there and listened to him explain how he wasn't getting what he wanted from me sexually.

He said she gave him what he wanted and then some. He said he felt like he was in

a porno when he was with her, and I wasn't "freaky" enough. The more he talked

the more I convinced myself it was my fault that he cheated. I told him I was

willing to stick it out, but I was not going to have sex with him again until I could

get the images out of my head of him licking, touching, and penetrating her. When

I was the side chick, I used to always wish I was the main chick or wife. Now that I

was the main chick it didn't feel good at all. My apologies to all the women I

betrayed by sleeping with their husbands or fiancé. How could he touch her and

lick her the same way he touched me. Heck, he was giving her more than he gave

me. Then I had to look at her 5 days a week at work, and she was a mean chick. It

didn't bother her at all that my heart was broken. She would even sing songs about

infidelity just to taunt me. I also heard through people at work that she laughed

about my pain and told people I was stupid for staying with him. All of this

motivated me to stay with him, because I was not going to let her have him. So

from that point, I made up my mind that I was going to do whatever freaky thing

Muhammad wanted me to do. Whatever it would take to satisfy him and make him

happy in the bed I will do it. She was the second woman he cheated on me with,

but she certainly wasn't the last. The reality is you can't satisfy someone that

doesn't have the ability to be satisfied. Muhammad slept with and tried to sleep with many other women at our job and probably outside of our job. And I don't think I found out about most of them until our relationship ended. Even today as we met he told me about more women he had slept with. Thank God for protection from AIDS, and any other diseases I could have gotten from him.

 We got past that cheating episode and things got back to a good place. We decided to visit his cousin who was a newlywed. They lived in Florida, so we also decided to go to Disney World while we were there. We were both excited about this vacation and we decided to rent a car and take that long drive so we could bond. The drive down was very good, but when we got there something changed. Now remember I told you, financially I took care of the bill most of the time. Yes, he contributed some, but he had a household to take care of, and two children. Well I spent most of my money for us on this trip, plus he told me to pay for his cousins' way into 2 Disney theme parks and I did. On the inside I was frustrated, but I also wanted to keep Muhammad happy because I felt if I ever denied him anything he would go cheat again. He also wanted me to dress a certain way, and this I wasn't willing to give in to. I was one of those victims of sexual abuse who was truly ashamed of her body. He would get very upset with me because I wouldn't wear short dresses, but I just couldn't bring myself to do it. I felt like I always had to have my body fully covered because maybe then a man would never force himself on me again.

Up to this point he had already done a number on my self-esteem from the cheating, telling me I wasn't good enough in the bed, and telling me I didn't look good enough. So the verbal, emotional, and mental abuse was very present in our relationship. A couple of nights we stayed with his family and one night he wanted to have sex. I told him no because I didn't feel comfortable having sex in that small apartment with his cousins possibly hearing us. I wanted to wait until we got to the hotel at Disney. I remember Muhammad being verbally aggressive, grabbing me around my mouth, and telling me I better have sex with him. Well of course my mind said he could probably find someone to sleep with here if I don't have sex with him. I complied, and I remember it was in that moment that things changed in our relationship and I needed to continue being the "compliant" girlfriend. And for the remainder of the trip I truly let him call all of the shots. Whatever he wanted or whatever he wanted to do, I went right along with it. On the outside it probably appeared like I was having a good time, but in reality, on the inside I wasn't. I remember a couple of times I couldn't hold it in and we had some arguments, and he would shut them down. At one point we were going at it so bad his cousin had to intervene and tell us we were both being petty.

I call myself an extreme introvert, although I didn't know this back then. I process everything within, so I had a lot of pinned up frustration and anger while we were in Florida. I knew the drive from Florida back to Cleveland was going to feel like we were driving from Maine to Seattle. There were so many things I wanted to get off my chest, but I knew it would turn into an argument, and there was no winning an argument with him. It makes sense, but I would surrender quickly when it came to confrontation with males, but I will argue with a female until I win. And just as I suspected, the ride home was very long, but it was the first incidence of physical abuse.............

We were in the car headed home and we had gotten into another argument. The next thing I knew, he snatched me by my hair, was verbally aggressive, and the stage was set. He made it very clear through his actions that I left him no choice but to resort to physical abuse in order to keep me in line. And in that moment I went right back to being a victim. It was like I was back in my comfort zone. How crazy was I to think I deserved "New Beginnings". No, Kacey, this is what you deserve, a controlling, verbally and physically abusive man. And for the next 10 months he did not disappoint me.

Once we returned from Florida it became a vicious cycle him cheating and beating, and sometimes we would have peace and fun. I became so comfortable in it and I truly believed the abuse was a sign of his love for me. We had some really good days, did a lot of good things together, but some of those good days I made it a point to mess them up. Yes there were days when things were going good and I would start an argument just so he would beat me. I was so used to chaos at this point in my life I didn't know how to handle nice Muhammad. And at the same time it was those good days that would keep me hopeful that the cheating and beating would stop. Then we decided to take this dysfunction to a whole new level, let's get married. So we went shopping for the engagement ring, and put it on my credit card. He started the payments and I ended up covering the rest. Then we began telling people about our engagement and planning our wedding. I am picking colors and shopping for wedding dresses. And I found the most beautiful wedding dress, and I couldn't wait to get married and have a wedding just like the one in my favorite movie, "The Best Man".

Well, the thrills of wedding planning didn't last long. Things became so hostile I finally decided I needed to talk to someone, so I told his mother about the abuse. Her response made me think I was an actress in a movie. The first thing she asked me was what did I do to provoke him to hit me, and whatever it was I needed to stop doing it. In that moment I felt so alone, if I wanted sympathy it was not going to come from her. As a matter of fact, not too long after my conversation with her, he choked me right outside of her house, and he ignored her when she was yelling for him to stop. His brother-in-law had to pry his hands from around my neck, and it took a long time for him to do it. I don't know why, but after that night, I was hoping his mother and brother-in-law would talk some sense into him and he would never hit me again, but I was wrong.

One of my male co-workers began flirting with me. He was so nice to me and we would have great conversations, especially about music. I found myself going to his cottage often because he was giving me what Muhammad wasn't giving me, and that was a caring, listening ear. So one day I decided to tell him about the abuse in my relationship. He asked me if I wanted him to say something to Muhammad, but I told him no because it would make things worse. I was only telling him about the abuse because I wanted some sympathy, not because I wanted out of the relationship. If he said something to Muhammad, and I had no plans on leaving him, then that would put me in serious danger. I can only imagine what that would have done to Muhammad's pride, and I'm sure I would have paid greatly for doing that. The guy I am talking about has the pseudonym "Safety" in my first book. Safety told me he would never treat me like that. He wanted me to leave Muhammad and give him a chance. I told him no, but I couldn't stop thinking about him, and I kept going to see him when I would go to work.

I continued hearing rumors at work about Muhammad cheating, and I just got so tired of it. It was then that I decided I would no longer be faithful, so I decided to cheat on Muhammad with Safety. We exchanged numbers and began talking on the phone. Safety was the kind of guy I only saw in movies, and never believed they existed in real life. I definitely didn't believe guys like him would be interested in me, so I decided to take it a step further and go on a date with him. Yes, this would be the ultimate revenge, if you are going to continue to cheat with all these women at work I am going to cheat with someone at work as well.

Safety and I went to the movies and we had such a good time I did not want the night to end. I couldn't take it a step further and have sex with Safety, he was too nice and I didn't want him to get caught up with me. The other reason I couldn't have sex with Safety had to do with me not wanting to disrespect Muhammad. Now I know many of you are thinking, why not, he sure was giving his goods to every female he could. I agree, but in my mind, he owned every part of me and had exclusive rights to me sexually. There was no way I could let another man have what belonged to Muhammad. Plus it's harder for a man to recover when his woman cheats because we give of ourselves emotionally and men mostly give of themselves strictly on a physical level. This is what I was telling myself back then that there was no way I could put Muhammad through that kind of pain. Plus, at that point I only went out on the date because I wanted Muhammad to feel a little bit of pain, and I wanted this to be the reason he would finally stop cheating and be faithful to me. If I had sex with Safety there is no way Muhammad would want to touch me sexually or marry me, and I definitely couldn't risk that. The ultimate goal was to get Muhammad to stop cheating, not for him to leave me.

Safety and I continued talking to one another and some serious feelings developed between us. I had to do something because I couldn't let things get too out of hand with him, because I still wanted to marry Muhammad. So one night Muhammad and I were at home, things were quiet, a little too quiet, so this was the perfect time to tell on myself. I was ready to suffer the consequences of cheating on him, but my hope was the end result would be Muhammad deciding to no longer cheat on me and we would live happily ever after. All I wanted was to be all that Muhammad needed and wanted. It is very difficult to think you are good enough when the person you love is more interested in how many more women he can get, then making sure you are happy. I was so desperate for Muhammad to stop cheating I was willing to do anything. Also, at this point in our relationship I had become so comfortable with the abuse and I felt like the abuse was his way of showing me love and since he was cheating so much I didn't feel loved so I needed that physical contact. Yes, abusing me proved his love to me and I needed to be loved on this night.

I had no idea my cheating was going to take the abuse to a whole new level. Right after I told him about the connection I made with Safety and that we had gone on a date, he lost it. Muhammad began breaking things and cussing me out.

He then began beating me and the next thing I knew he pulled out several guns and asked me why he shouldn't use them on me. He held me hostage in the apartment for a long time, and I remember just sitting on the couch afraid to breathe. Recently, Muhammad asked me when did I stop loving him, and I told him it was on this night when he held me hostage at gun point. I had become used to being physically abused, and had truly become numb to it. But this was the first time one of my abusers actually pulled a gun on me. Fear kicked in and love was gone in an instant. I don't recall exactly how many hours he held me hostage, but I do know it seemed like forever. This was truly traumatizing, and one of the contributors of my memory loss.

After that day, I continued talking to Safety, but I had to do it very discretely. And my plan definitely backfired because Muhammad took his cheating to a whole new level. Yes, he continued to cheat and spend money on other women. So my plan to get him to stop cheating didn't work, I guess I shouldn't have expected him to stop. I mean, up to this point I pretty much let him get away with it, time after time. Why should he stop when he could have his cake and eat it too.

He sent a dozen roses to a woman who worked in the same cottage with me, and we were even working the same shift on this particular day. I had this bad feeling they were from him, and she wouldn't admit it with her mouth, but I could see it in her eyes. My heart sank into my stomach and I truly felt like I had lost

Muhammad. How bold was that, you threaten me and tell me I better not cheat again, and you cheat on me with someone I work with directly and have formed a bond with. Having sex with other women is one thing, but sending roses is intimate. This meant he had to have some real feelings for her. Plus, this woman was already in an on and off relationship with one of Muhammad's closest friends. I don't know where the courage came from, but this was the final straw for me. I couldn't do it anymore, and not only did I break up with him, but I sent his friend a dozen roses as payback.

Muhammad was not willing to let go so easily. He was calling me, showing up at the apartment, but I wouldn't give in. Safety and I began talking on a regular basis, but I wanted it to remain a secret because I didn't want Muhammad to find out. Somehow he did find out and I have no idea how he found out. One night at work he wanted to talk to me, but I told him I didn't want to talk. I was on my way to Safety's cottage to visit with him, and Muhammad followed me. When we entered the cottage, Muhammad pulled a hand gun out on me, and I ran upstairs and he followed. Since he followed me, and I didn't want anyone else to get hurt, I decided to comply and talk to him.

He told me to get in his car and he drove me around the neighborhood with the gun to my head questioning me about Safety. Once again the fear was so overwhelming, I was saying anything to him, in hopes that he would calm down. I cannot remember anything I said to him, I just remember the gun touching my head the whole time, and me wondering where are the police when you need them. He was driving at high rates of speed and it scared me because one wrong move and he could accidentally pull the trigger. He was so out of control, I now know it was only God that kept him from pulling that trigger. He drove me back to my car, and I couldn't wait to get in it, alive, and go home.

When I got home, I called Safety to tell him what happened. He asked me if I called the police and I told him no. For some reason, no matter how much they beat us, or how close we come to losing our life, we still protect them. Safety had a mutual friend talk to me while he excused himself off the phone. I later found out Safety called the police from another phone, told them what happened, and asked them to patrol my parking lot to ensure Muhammad wasn't there. Safety then talked to me until I was ready to go to sleep.

The next morning I got ready for work and proceeded out of my apartment with all my guards totally down. As I walked out of my building, all I remember is Muhammad coming from behind the door attacking me. I saw a woman walking through the parking lot and I screamed for her to please help me. She turned away as if she didn't hear me, but the good thing is it distracted Muhammad long enough to give me a head start to my car. I jumped in fast enough to lock the door, and he jumped on the hood of my car and I drove off anyway. I was headed for the police station right up the street, and as I sat at the red light, there was an image in my head of him shooting me as I ran into the police station. A voice, (which I now know was the Holy Spirit), told me to go to work. I initially questioned it, but I went to work, with Muhammad right behind me. I pulled into the parking lot and ran into my cottage, locked it, and told my supervisor to please call the police, because Muhammad was trying to kill me. Muhammad circled around the cottage on foot yelling for me to come outside. The police finally showed up, cuffed him, questioned me, found the gun, and took him to jail.

Muhammad was in jail, and Safety jumped right in to fill the void, and I was so happy he was there. Safety was the man you literally only see in movies. I know I have said this before, but he is truly one of those men who will always hold a special place in my heart because he had nothing but love and respect for me. One day we were talking on the phone about our likes and dislikes and I told him white roses were my favorite flowers, and a couple days later I came home to 2 dozen, white roses sitting outside my apartment door. He was everything I dreamed of in a man, and I truly felt like I was living a fairytale. Then Muhammad was released on bail, and guess what, I ended up right back in his arms. Yes, I let him talk his way right back into my life. Statistics say a victim of domestic violence will leave 5-7 times and return, before they leave for good. The way he talked to me made me truly believe he had changed, I can drop the charges, and we can move on as scheduled with our wedding plans. We made love as if nothing happened and for over a week things were great. Well, before we could walk down the aisle, the verbal abuse started again, and threats of further abuse, so I had to call the police. The Prosecutor asked if I was in agreement with a plea deal which would give him 2 years and that way I could avoid sitting through a trial. I agreed, Muhammad got the 2 years, and I could finally move on with Safety.

Things were so great with him, but as great as Safety was, he wasn't great enough to erase all the damage from years of domestic violence and low self-esteem. When you have spent about 8 years of your life being verbally and physically abused, it is a great challenge to truly believe someone great like Safety wants anything to do with you. I felt so unworthy of all the love he was showing me, and because of that, I called him one night and told him I couldn't continue seeing him because he was just too good for me, and he deserved better than me. I let 1 of the 3 best men to ever walk into my life go because I thought I only deserved guys that would abuse me, and not guys that would treat me like a Queen.

At that point in my life I probably would have gone back to Muhammad if he wasn't in prison. Why do we go back? One of the reasons is because going back is familiar. Even though our lives are at risk, in the back of our minds we truly don't believe he is really going to kill us, because he needs us. He may beat me, but it would never go as far as death, because who would take care of all of his needs.

Sometimes we go back because the relationship wasn't always bad, and there were some really great times in the beginning. In the back of our mind we are hoping he will go back to being that prince charming that got us in the first place. Also, I don't know about other victims of abuse, but I also had made up in my mind I would stay until he did get better, because I had invested too much time and effort in him, and there was no way I would let him go. What if he gets himself together I want to be the one to reap the benefits of him being in a better place, and there is no way I'm going to let another woman reap those benefits.

The reasons I mentioned above are referred to as "secondary gains". A secondary gain is a reason I stay in a situation that is good for me or not good for me. So if I'm in an abusive situation and my abuser is paying all my bills and taking care of my kids, those are my secondary gains and the reasons I put up with the abuse, because I need someone else to do those things because I don't believe I can do them for myself. And these are some of the reasons we stay or we keep going back. If you are currently in an abusive situation, ask yourself right now, whether you are the victim or the abuser, what are your secondary gains?

In the midst of the abuse we don't see ourselves as being worthy of anything better, and we believe this is how relationships are supposed to function. We are no different than the person who is addicted to drugs, alcohol, gambling, etc. We are addicted to the man we are with, and we are addicted to being loved, unfortunately we believe that love is expressed through being controlled and abused.

Chapter 3: Journey of Healing

After I broke up with Safety, I got into two meaningless relationships. I found out Safety got engaged, and that's when it hit me that I made the biggest mistake of my life by letting him go. I cried for days and couldn't eat or sleep. One day as I was wallowing in my pain, I decided I was going to marry the next man I met. If Safety can get married, then I will get married too. Either marriage will help me get over Safety or maybe Safety will not get married if he finds out I am getting married and we can reunite!

Safety got married in June, I got married in August, and 4 months into my marriage I realized I still had feelings for Safety and my marriage was not going to cure that. I began acting out in my marriage by picking fights with my husband and just being unbearable. My marriage lasted only 2 years, really 1 year because it took a year to finalize the divorce. One tremendous blessing came from the marriage and that is our wonderful son who is now 12. My son is one of the main reasons I have changed my life around. My son is a true inspiration to me because he makes me want to be the best person and mother I can be. I don't want to talk about being a good person I want to be a living example for him.

After my divorce I got involved in more relationships that I should not have gotten involved in. One was very emotionally and verbally abusive, but the sex was so good I couldn't walk away from him. We had been friends for 4 years, and I never knew this side of him existed. Sometimes you don't know a person until you sleep with them. Once again I am involved with someone I work with. He questioned just about every move I made, which caused me to walk on egg shells most of the relationship. If I was talking to a male co-worker he would accuse me of cheating. He would talk down to me and make me feel like I didn't have much intelligence. I am one of those people who loves small things. I don't ask for much, but when I do I have high expectations to receive it. For example, during our relationship he never expressed how he felt about me. With Valentine's Day around the corner I asked him if he could please just get me a card and write on the inside how he feels about me. I told him I didn't want candy, flowers, or anything else, I just wanted that card. Well he began yelling at me and telling me how selfish I was for asking him for anything, and I should let him get me what he wants to get me. Before I knew it I was crying and apologizing to him for being selfish, and he decided he was not going to give me anything for Valentine's Day. I still gave him his gift anyway, two tickets to see our professional basketball team. I put up with this for the 6 months we were together, and when I look back the sex was not worth it, it was the best I had ever had, but not worth the stress.

Then a divine appointment with God gave me the strength I needed to walk away from the most amazing sex I have ever had in my life. This divine encounter with God opened my eyes to so many truths about me and those truths were:

1. I needed God desperately
2. I was a broken woman that needed to be healed.
3. I was not just a victim in my relationships, but I also contributed to some of the chaos.
4. My self-esteem was very low, and it caused me to believe I was only good for sex.
5. My promiscuity was a sin, and God's plan is for me to only have sex within marriage.
6. I needed to take a break from men.
7. I needed counseling.
8. I needed to be introduced to the Kacey Alston God created me to be.
9. I needed to discover and experience what true joy and happiness is because I had never truly experienced that.

God is so faithful and so loving that He placed me in a church with a Pastor who was anointed to speak to broken women like me and also a counseling department that was run by a Licensed Professional Counseling. Individual and

Group Counseling was available, and I took full advantage of both, and this is when my healing process began. Our Pastor was very intentional about telling us the importance of developing our own personal relationship with the Lord, which led me to reading the bible daily and praying daily. I told God I wanted to try to live my life according to His word. The way I had been living my life was not working, and I might as well give God's way a try. I also promised God that I would not have sex again until I got married. It has been over 10 years, and I am so glad God did not tell me it would be this long because I don't know how willing I would have been, LOL! I'm not going to talk too much about my journey of abstinence. But I would love for you to read my books Deliverance from Sexual Sin and Deliverance from Sexual Sin 2. In these 2 books I go into detail about how I have maintained abstinence for over 10 years.

Once I told God I was ready to live my life for Him, it was like I became invisible. For the first year and a half not one man showed any interest in me. This took some time to get used to because I went from always needing a man, to not even having a man to talk to on the phone. I needed the break because it gave me so much one on one time with God. While reading His word, I discovered what real love is, and it definitely isn't sex or abuse.

Then God began speaking to me in many different forms and I looked forward to spending time with him every morning and evening. I felt like I truly owed God all of me, because He truly saved my life. I should not have made it out of those physically abusive relationships alive, but I know God kept me alive for many reasons and one reason was so Muhammad and I could write this book.

I finally decided to be brave and take advantage of the counseling services at my church. The first group being offered was for women who had been in domestic violence relationships. I went into the group with a negative mind set because I just knew whoever was running the group would have no idea what it is like to be beaten and in fear of losing your life. Well, I was totally wrong, because the first day of our group the facilitator shared with us how she was in an eleven year, abusive relationship that almost ended in her death. This was a huge relief, and I felt more comfortable to share my story. My journey of healing began with my relationship with God, and continued in this group. It was truly a blessing to be with other women who had been in similar situations. Group counseling can be so beneficial, because it helps you to know you are not alone, you are not stupid, and there are other people out there with a similar struggle.

The hardest part for me was facing the fact that I was just as much of a problem in these relationships, as my abuser. Now I am not saying that my abusers had a right to abuse me, because they did not, and I am also not saying it's my fault they abused me. I am saying I had to recognize the reasons why I was attracted to abusive men, and why I stayed in abusive situations, and why I was comfortable being a victim. Yes, I was very comfortable being a victim, in my mind abuse=love.

Why was I attracted to abusers, I will begin in my childhood, and I promise I am not playing the blame game. There are some theorists who believe our childhood has nothing to do with the choices we make later in life, and they do counseling with people in the "here and now", and refuse to do any work with their clients regarding their past. I am not in agreement with that and counseling helped me to know why. There were people and events that happened in my life that contributed to my belief system and how I saw the world.

I come from a long line of Christians, and religious Christians. What do I mean by "Religious Christians?" I mean Christians that were mostly concerned with following rules and traditions. Those of you who are 40+ years old like me, were likely raised by parents that were all about rule following and the famous words, "Do as I say and not as I do." Adults weren't interested in our opinions, we were kids and we were only supposed to know what we were taught at home, school, and church. Oh, and adults were always right even when they were wrong. In my household all of your life decisions were made for you in a controlling manner. Our parents raised us the best they knew how, and I am truly thankful for my parents. I have learned from being a parent myself that we parent our children based on how we were parented, life experiences, and the world around us.

Being a victim of sexual, verbal, and physical abuse, being controlled, having very little self-esteem, contributed to me viewing the world and the people in it, in a certain way. I had no idea I had a voice and definitely didn't think people cared about what I had to say. I had no idea my opinion mattered, and I had no idea I could say "no" to a man without consequences. I did not think I was pretty and I wanted to be liked by someone so desperately. So if being liked means being controlled, beat up, and used for sex then I will accept that as long as you don't leave me. Back then I wasn't aware of this, it was just a natural way of life for me. Counseling helped me to see how all of these things contributed to my bad choices and decisions.

I was a wounded individual and it began so early in my life. I had no idea how wounded I was, and this made the early stages of counseling a challenge. Yes, it was a challenge because I believed my way of life and my relationships were okay. I am so glad I took the group for survivors of domestic violence because now my eyes are wide open as to why I found myself in the cycle of abuse.

I am fully aware that many of you reading this book may not be spiritual, so I am going to explain some things in spiritual and non-spiritual language. The healing process answered the question of why I was so attracted to and attractive to abusive men. Many of us believe attraction is more external than internal, and I am a firm believer that attraction is more internal then external. I was just explaining to a friend yesterday that our first attraction to a person is internal. He strongly disagreed with me, because he believes physical attraction is the first attraction, and we were able to agree to disagree, but this is my philosophy. The reason I believe the internal attraction happens first, is for this reason. If I physically desire men who are tall, with facial hair, and a medium build, and physical attraction is the first attraction, then I will be attracted to and interested in getting to know every man that fit that description. However, in reality, there have been many men who fit that description and I walked right by them without a second look. In reality there were only a few guys that I was involved with who fit that physical description, but most of them fit the description of abuser. When I first saw them I had no idea they were abusive, but within me I was so drawn to them, it was almost magnetic. Have you ever said, "I am so attracted to him/her and I don't know why, I just can't get enough of them?" The reason is because that person meets your inner most needs. The needs could range from the need to be controlled to the need to be loved. In counseling we say "healthy attracts healthy, and unhealthy attracts unhealthy". How in the world could I be attracted at first site to men who were either controlling or abusive, 98% of the time? That had nothing to do with physical attraction and everything to do with my inner self. Givers are attracted to takers, introverts are attracted to extroverts, selfish people are attracted to unselfish people, controlling people attract very submissive people, and on and on. Now I'm not saying this happens 100% of the time, but I do believe that inner attraction happens 99.9% of the time when we meet someone. Just take a moment to think about every person you were drawn to or you had a relationship with. I am so certain you will agree with me, and I believe there is only a small amount of you who will agree with my friend that physical attraction happens first. I am never one to push religion on anyone, but this is truly evidence that we are spiritual beings, and we truly attract that which is within us, or the needs we desire within.

Those of us who are spiritual must recognize church attendance and serving in ministry is not the cure for this. If we come to Christ wounded on the inside, and we don't feed our spirit the word of God, we don't spend time with God, and we don't get our healing, we will continue to attract wounded people. And we can always measure how healthy we are within, by the people we attract in our lives. I had to realize I needed to get rid of as much of that pain out of my mind, my spirit, and my heart, if I wanted to attract healthy men. I also needed to learn to forgive others and myself for my past. Unforgiveness keeps us stuck in the past and the present, and in the next chapter I will talk about the power of forgiveness.

So not only did I participate in the group for survivors of domestic violence, I also participated in a group for women who had been raped and or molested, a group about grief, a group for women with love and sex addictions, and a group for women to learn how to establish boundaries in their relationships. When a person has been sexually or physically abused, they have learned through those interactions that they must make themselves available to people whenever, or they build Fort Knox around themselves and won't make themselves available to anybody. Even in other relationships such as working relationships, church relationships, many of these people don't think they can say no, and they will do whatever people ask them to do, or refuse to do anything. Then I had to dig even deeper in my individual counseling sessions, and that was a lot of hard work, but it was worth it!

I began doing all of this work about 8 years ago, and I am still doing the work. You can't undo 32 years of dysfunction overnight, and because I have been healed in many areas of my life, I want to continue my journey of healing. As I stated earlier I am in school obtaining my Master's in counseling, and I am getting even more healing through this program. For the first full year of my Master's Program we had to be clients in group counseling, and I was glad I was able to get more healing.

Now I am going to be very transparent because I don't want anyone getting the impression that I am an expert about what I am writing about, because I am not. I will promote God and the power of His healing, and counseling, however, it is a process. There are some things God healed me from in an instant, and there are some things that I am still in the process of getting my deliverance and healing. What did He instantly deliver and heal me of: my addiction to alcohol, drugs, and sex. I haven't had a drink or a drug in over 14 years, and I haven't had sex in over 10 years, and that includes masturbation and oral sex. Those addictions kept me stuck in unhealthy relationships and I am so thankful He has disciplined me enough to say no to all of them.

Now, in what areas am I still unhealthy and in need of daily prayer and healing? I still attract, and I am somewhat attracted to men who are mentally and emotionally unavailable, men who are controlling, and men with attachment issues. And I also suffer from symptoms of anxiety, depression, and P.T.S.D. and they are all a result of the many years of abuse and trauma I suffered.

Wow, I can't believe I just shared that, but I feel I needed to, because there are long term effects victims of domestic violence, abandonment, and sexual abuse suffer with. Your long term effects may be different, but trust me when I tell you, when you make the decision to seek God for your healing it will be worth it. Now I have not been in a physically abusive relationship since my relationship with Muhammad, and that was 16 years ago. However, I have been in relationships in which the men displayed signs that they could become abusive, and the difference now is, I don't stick around. About 7 years ago I fell hard for a man, and he was emotionally unavailable and was somewhat aggressive, but never abusive. It was hard to walk away from him, so I literally had to pray my way out of the relationship. That is healing for me, because as I told you I was a woman who was very comfortable allowing a man to control me, use me, and abuse me.

My prayers now are centered on being healthy enough so I can attract men who are emotionally and mentally available. I want to be attracted to men who are not afraid of healthy attachments, and men who do not want to control me. I also have abandonment issues and tend to attract men, who like to abandon relationships, and I am definitely tired of encountering those types of men, and I have been consistently praying about that. I will never let another man put his hands on me, so it is important for me to continue my healing process. Now when I meet someone and I see these unhealthy characteristics in them I make the decision not to continue seeing that person. This is also a message to me to continue my journey of inner healing. Now the reality is any person we marry will have issues, the key is knowing what issues we are equipped to handle.

It is my prayer that Muhammad and I have the privilege to travel the world to talk to men and women about breaking the cycle of domestic violence. For that reason I am not going to go into too many details about my healing process, because I want to be able to tell you in person! I will say this to all victims and perpetrators of domestic violence. Whenever you decide to end the cycle in your life, please develop a relationship with Jesus Christ, seek Him for healing, and continue that journey as long as possible. And please try not to jump into any relationships, because time to yourself is important, at least in the beginning of your healing process.

In summary, don't listen to people telling you how stupid you are for staying in the relationship. Don't listen to people telling you that you should rot in jail for the rest of your life for abusing someone. Some jail time may be necessary, but not the rest of your life. Whether victim or perpetrator, God is listening if you desire healing, seek Him for that! I am a firm believer that when we know better, we do better. Muhammad and I are living proof of this!

Chapter 4: Forgiveness

"Forgiveness: The action or process of forgiving or being forgiven. Synonyms: pardon, absolution, exoneration, remission, dispensation, indulgence, clemency, mercy."

The synonyms say it all! Forgiveness is a word some people don't even allow in their vocabulary. Forgiveness is a word that we can use freely, but we can also refuse to acknowledge. Forgiveness can be easy at times, and other times it can be one of the hardest things we do.

"Then Peter came to Jesus and asked, Lord, how many times shall I forgive my brother or sister who sins against me? Up to seven times? Jesus answered, I tell you, not seven times, but seventy-seven times." Matthew 18:21-22. We are instructed by God to forgive, and yes He understands it's not always easy. Take a moment and think of the worst thing you have ever done in your life. When you asked God to forgive you, He didn't say no, maybe, I'm going to hold a grudge forever. No He said, "If you confess your sins I am faithful and just to forgive and cleanse you from all unrighteousness." 1John1:9 (paraphrase). If God can forgive us over and over, there is no reason we shouldn't forgive people over and over. He didn't say it would always be easy, He didn't say it wouldn't be painful, He just instructed us to do it.

There was a time in my life that I hated a particular person so much I wanted them to die. Yes, for about five minutes I thought about how wonderful my life would be if this person was no longer on this earth. Then I came to my senses and decided I just wanted to hate this person the rest of my life and I'm not referring to Muhammad. However, when it came to Muhammad I didn't want to hate him, but I definitely didn't want to forgive him.

About 8 years ago I watched a sermon titled, "The Bait of Satan", by John Bevere, he also wrote a book on the sermon. This sermon/book was all about forgiveness. After listening to this sermon I was in tears, and I was begging God to forgive me for all the people I haven't forgiven. Over a year later, I started thinking about Muhammad, and at this point it has been 9 years since he went to prison. I didn't understand why I was thinking about him, until I heard the Lord say, "forgive him". Okay Lord, I know I felt bad for harboring unforgiveness, but do I really need to forgive him? Why should I have to forgive him? He doesn't deserve my forgiveness, he tried to kill me. Yes I've done some things that didn't deserve forgiveness, but never anything as bad as he did, please God, I don't want to do this. I continued to question God, and he remained silent.

Finally, I prayed and I told God, "I release all unforgiveness for Muhammad right now, and Lord if I am still holding on to unforgiveness, I give it to you please take it." I actually felt a weight lifted off me. I know many of us hold on to unforgivness because we think forgiving someone means that person gets a pass for what they did. Forgiveness has nothing to do with that person, and everything to do with us being free, and for those of us who are Christians it strengthens our relationship with God. "For if you forgive other people when they sin against you, your heavenly father will also forgive you. But if you do not forgive others their sins, your Father will not forgive our sins." Matthew 6:14-15. If I want to be forgiven by God, then I need to forgive others. And as I stated, I felt a weight lifted off me. Unforgiveness can affect us mentally and physically.

I forgave Muhammad and I'm actually glad I did. Several months after I told God I was letting go of my unforgiveness for Muhammad, The Lord said something to me that shocked me. The Lord instructed me to go tell Muhammad to his face that I had forgiven him. Did I hear you clearly God? Here we go again! There is no way I can ever look into the face of the man who verbally and physically abused me and also threatened to end my life. For weeks I refused to do this, and during those weeks I had no peace.

Once again God wins, and I decide to obey. Muhammad had opened a restaurant that is named after his mother, and I walked into the restaurant and asked for him. I stood nervously waiting for him to come out front, and as he approached me, a flood of emotions took over. I told him I had come to let him know I had forgiven him, and there was a look of disbelief on his face. He then went on to tell me that he had been praying for this day to happen. He gave praises to God for answering his prayers and he thanked me for forgiving him.

As I left the restaurant I told God that I have no idea why he had me do that, but I am glad I obeyed. Five years later Muhammad reached out to me on social media, and I did not respond to him, forgiveness doesn't mean I have to talk to you if I don't want to. About a year later he reached out again on social media, and I finally responded. He thanked me and informed me that his wife had passed away and wanted to know if I could refer him and his children to someone for counseling. I expressed my condolences, gave him the contact information, and told him I would be praying for them.

A year later he reached out to me on social media and asked me if I wanted to co-author this book with him. Initially I wanted to say heck no, but I was nice and told him I would pray about it. Now I will be honest and say I had no intention on praying about it, but I found myself praying about it. Right after I prayed, I got the answer in the form of the title of the book. What????? God you really want me to do this???? I informed Muhammad that I was all in and that we would communicate through email. I was not comfortable enough to give him my number or see him in person again. He agreed, but it didn't last long.

Yes, trying to write a book with someone via email presented challenges, so we scheduled our first face to face meeting. Sitting across from him was so awkward. My anxiety was very high and I was very uncomfortable. However, it turned out to be an amazing experience. I didn't realize how much I forgot about our relationship until we had this meeting. I have come to understand our brain doesn't always record traumatic events.

Muhammad reminded me of the time we drove to Niagara Falls for a weekend. It was a wonderful, romantic weekend, and there was no drama. I do remember it being extra special, because at the time and even now, Muhammad is one of only two men I have gone on vacation with. Muhammad and I had a lot of good times, unfortunately the bad times were so big they outweighed the good times. That one face to face meeting turned into many, and with each meeting I was able to let my guard down, and I now feel very comfortable being around him.

What's great about us writing this book is it allows me to continue my healing process. My focus is less on all the bad things he did to me, and more on who I am as a result of our relationship. Muhammad gave me so much insight into what it was like to be in a relationship with me. Not once did he blame me for his actions, but he did let me know there were days I was a very difficult person to deal with. I can believe that, and Muhammad I hope you have forgiven me for the role I played in our relationship being tumultuous.

I want everyone reading this book to understand what I just said. There is nothing a victim of domestic violence can do to MAKE an abuser, abuse them. An abuser makes a CHOICE when they decide to abuse. I don't want anyone thinking I believe it was my fault Muhammad abused me. What I want him to forgive me for are the days when things were going well for us, and I would decide to start an argument or make him mad for no reason. Well unconsciously there was a reason I started those arguments and that was because I truly needed the chaos of our relationship because I was used to it, and quiet was unfamiliar and scary for me. I know this may be difficult for many to comprehend, but we already know I wasn't in a healthy place so it only makes sense that dysfunction had become functional for me. The more and more we have worked on this book, the more thankful to God I am for leading me to forgive.

To all abusers and all victims of domestic violence, healing is crucial, and forgiveness is just as crucial. Healing is crucial so we don't continue the cycle of abuse. If you notice, I continually hooked up with abusive guys because I wasn't ready to heal. I will repeat forgiveness is for you not for the person you are forgiving. Forgiveness helps us to let go and move on without holding a grudge. Forgiveness does not mean we have to reconcile and get back together. Muhammad and I both know we had our chance at love 17 years ago, and this book is not about us trying love with each other again, we are both on our own separate journeys. Now that doesn't mean some couples won't get their healing together and mend their relationship. I would never tell a couple they shouldn't get back together, that's between you and God. I am saying healing and forgiveness must occur regardless. And it may not ever be safe for you to be around your abuser, but you don't need to interact with them in order to heal, and you can go through the process of forgiveness with God and/or through counseling. I was determined to get my healing whether I spoke to Muhammad again, or not. I am just thankful God led me to forgive him so we could do this project. I pray this book will save some from abusive relationships, deliver people from abusive relationships, draw some people to heal and forgive, and most importantly draw limitless amounts of people to a relationship with Christ!

FORGIVENESS!!!!!!!!!!!!!!!! PASS IT ON!!!!!!!!!!!!!!!!!!!!!!!!!

Conclusion

To all the men and women who are currently a victim of a domestic violence relationship, I want you to know I feel your pain, and I want you to know God loves you so much. I am not going to tell you to leave your relationship, because that could put you in a very dangerous situation and I don't know your story. It is my prayer that you will desire a healthy relationship someday and you will do everything within your power to ensure that happens, and God will do what you can't.

And I want to say this because many believe a relationship is only abusive if the person hits you. If the person you are in a relationship with puts you down, calls you out of your name, causes you to believe you can never do anything right or measure up, and if they are always keeping tabs on you, always wanting to know where you are, that is verbal and emotional abuse. That can definitely be classified as an abusive relationship and you definitely want to consider counselor or asking yourself if this is a relationship you should be in. I pray my words and Muhammad's words give you the strength to look at yourself and say, "I deserve better."

You are not stupid, you are not weak you are a butterfly who hasn't discovered its purpose YET! I want you to know there is a door to freedom whenever you want to open it and walk through it! As I stated earlier, statistics say a victim leaves and returns to their abusers up to 5-7 times before they decide to leave for good. You are not in this alone there are others like you who are still in it. My advice is, don't leave until you have a safe place to go. Having them arrested and protection orders are the first steps. However, if you don't have that safe place to go, a protection order won't stop them from coming to you and killing you. If you have the ability, change your number, that way you are not tempted to respond to their pleas for you to come back. Some phone carriers will do it for free if you are fleeing an abuser or being stalked. I have had to take advantage of this free service a couple of times. And as soon as possible begin counseling, in order to begin the process of breaking the cycle, and for healing to occur.

One last thing, if you make the decision to leave, may I please suggest that you don't tell your abuser. I am not saying your abuser will end your life if you do tell them, but do you want to take that chance. I want to make it clear I am not telling you to leave your relationship. However, if you decide to leave please be careful and follow some of these tips I have given if you choose.

To all former victims, I thank God you made it out of your domestic violence relationship alive. I pray you have already gotten counseling, if not please consider it. Heal in order to break the cycle. Please don't be like me and miss out on a good person just because you don't believe you are good enough for them. Become that healthy person who attracts healthy people! Remember there are warning signs to abusive relationships. If a person wants to be exclusive with you soon after you meet them, be very careful! I'm not saying that equals abuse but it is a sign. If they always want to know where you are, be careful! If the person calls you all the time, questions you about why you haven't called them back, or gets mad when they can't get in touch with you, please be very careful! Ladies I know sometimes we think it's cute when he ALWAYS wants to be with us, and when he is ALWAYS keeping tabs on us, but it's a clear sign of abandonment issues, and it sometimes leads to controlling, abusive behaviors. Please don't overlook these warning signs, and proceed in the relationship slowly, and cautiously. You don't want to end up in another abusive relationship….. And please, if you haven't accepted Christ as your savior, please consider it! I love you and I am praying for you!

To all who are currently or have abused the one you love, I refuse to judge you. I am a firm believer that people who know better in their head and their heart, do better. I truly believe your head and or your heart is wounded. Wounded heads and hearts don't operate properly, and they convince us to harm others, whether it's through our words or actions. I am not excusing your behaviors, because no one has the right to inflict abusive harm on another human being. However, I understand why you have decided to control and abuse your loved one.

I understand you saw one of your parents abuse the other one, or even you, and you believed it was okay for you to do the same. I understand when your father told you it was okay for you to hit your woman in order to keep her in line you believed it. I understand you saw your mother verbally and physically abuse men and you view all men as weak and you refuse to be the one abused so you become the abuser. I understand you being abandoned as a child lead you to make the decision to control and obsess over any person you are in a relationship with because you are scared of being abandoned again.

Do you realize the power you use to abuse others is the same power you can use to walk away from an abusive situation? Do the hard work in counseling, and develop healthy intimate relationships with others. Yes, it's going to be difficult to face the pain of your past, and face who you are right now! I guarantee you it will all be worth it! Jesus didn't take the beating so you could spend your life dishing out the beatings to others. It's never too late to make that change. Muhammad is a great example of someone who made that change, and he didn't do it alone. God and others have contributed to his transformation, and God can do the same for you! And unfortunately sometimes that transformation only comes when you spend time in prison thinking about how you could have done things differently.

Whether your transformation comes from going to prison or walking away from the relationship, it is my prayer one or the other happens before someone ends up dead. It doesn't take long for a choke, or a beating to end up in death. We have lost enough people due to domestic violence please don't be the next one to add another person to those statistics. You are worthy of a healthy relationship and it's not too late for you to get all the help you need. I love you and I'm praying for you!

HIS SIDE

Introduction

One of the hardest things to do growing up is finding who you are. The best way to do it is to just let experience be your guide. Impatience will drive you crazy. To some it may be a little easier, but for me it took 45 years for me to get a clue. I am still learning more about myself each day. Now I'm at the point where I'm enjoying the ride, instead of trying to rush life. When you experience so much negativity in your life it tends to become your life. You walk around with this black cloud over your head, and expect every situation to have a negative outcome. This makes daily living hard to bear, you can get lost in all of this. For me it took a strong will and deep spirituality to overcome this everyday depression, and pinned up anger. A lot has changed for me. Even though things are not where I need or want them to be, it's just where it's supposed to be. Happiness is finally here! The reason it took me so long is because I did not put God first, the moment I did my life change drastically. I always believed that I was the master of my life, and that God was just the master of the universe, no!!! He is the master of all.

I am a 45 year old black man who has been wandering through it almost carelessly, with no true goals, and basically living day by day. I never knew my purpose and I never knew what direction to go. I grew up in a single parent home with my mother, and my dad was married and had another family out of state. My mother was a very loving and caring woman who had little or no self-esteem or self -worth, plus she struggled with drug and alcohol addiction. Now this may seem like a bad way to have grown up, but somehow I managed to become a good human being, with a few character flaws. My reason for writing this book is to confront myself and to show my growth. You've probably heard the term "from rags to riches, and back to rags", Well this concept can be used to describe my life, but it would be "from good to bad, back to great". It may sound silly but it describes my character, and my spirit.

It is my sincerest hope that this missive reaches a young man or a young woman who may be experiencing the same or something similar to me and Kacey's situation, in order to help them before things go too far and someone is severely hurt, dead, or imprisoned for a very long time. I have learned forgiveness and closure are very important when it comes to the healing process, and I pray you feel the same way as you read my side.

Chapter 5: About Me

I lay here sleepy and tired, but unable to fall asleep. My mind is racing a million

miles a minute because I always think of her, her being my ex-wife. I think of the

things I did wrong in my marriage, the things I wish I could change. How could I

have treated the woman I loved and the mother of my two beautiful children that

way? I wish I could apologize, but I can't because she's gone, and by gone I mean

she's dead. So no retribution here, I am forever haunted by my lack of being a

good husband. Then I go from one thought to another in a matter of seconds,

because I am unable to stay focused on one thing in particular. I feel like I'm

suffering a slow torture, I am almost dead inside. The ones that keep me focused

and able to see clearly, are these beautiful children, but even they can't fix my self

-inflicted torture. Why do I endure so much pain, and still find a way to function

day to day without cracking from the pressure of my past existence and peril. I

have truly been plagued by my past indiscretions.

Then I think of another her, her being my former lover. I know it's been said to

forgive yourself for your disservice to not only you, but the people you genuinely

care and have cared about. However, this is hard when your spirituality is weak.

(Her) wrote about her life in a book, and of course a section in the book contained

her experience with me. I was a terrible person to her on more than one occasion, and for this I am forever ashamed. How do you forgive such atrocities? How do you move on to be a better person when you've hurt the ones you truly love? I want her to know I'm a better person because of her, and I want her to know that I truly did love her, and still do. I could never be that man again because I hate him and despise him. I could never share my life with her again and I know this. I just want to be true friends with her, however, I also know this will never come to pass.

My past does not let go, it forever haunts me to the point I can't sleep. I have prayed and prayed and prayed, and I think God wants me to hurt more, because of the pain I've dished out. I just want to share this with young or older men and women who are going through the same things I have, or to possibly keep someone from going down that same road I have travelled. If I can reach one person and keep that person from going down the wrong road, I will feel accomplished.

My earliest memories are of my mother and grandmother. My father was around a little, but all I can remember is not being around him that much. The two ladies I mentioned pretty much raised me and molded me into the man I have become, raising me with old fashion values and ways. One thing I remember most is my grandmother always telling me never to be abusive to a woman mentally or physically. She pounded this into me almost on a daily basis. I was also told that I should be married before having sex, and that I should get married young, and so all of my childhood I lived by this. My mother trained me to believe that children were to be taken care of by their parents, and once they were adults they were to take care of their parents. Because of this I spent many days wondering how I would be able to manage taking care of a family. My mother was poor, and had jobs in take-out restaurants and the pay was crappy. Because of this we didn't have much but we managed to survive by living in low income housing, specifically the projects.

I came up in an era where it was fashionable to give your woman a rap in the mouth if she got out of line. My mother, grandmothers, and most women I knew had experienced some form of this physical abuse from a man. One example of abuse was of my grandmother, who was forced to have rough sex with my grandfather. She pounded in my head to be gentle with a woman because it could do damage to a woman's body. This form of abuse led to her having a hysterectomy. It wasn't until I got older that I realized what, and why she was saying this. One of my first fights as a kid was with a girl. Of course my first loss came at the hands of this female Mike Tyson, and I went home crying. My mother slapped me and told me to go back out there and kick her behind or she was going to kick mine. Needless to say my second loss came from this same girl. At this point, because of teasing and ridicule from my boys, it became my mission to kick a girl's ass. See how the cycle starts sometimes? My mentality was being manipulated even as a young boy all the way into my adulthood. It was about power and control. Keeping a woman's self-esteem low meant she would never be strong enough to beat you, or to leave you.

In my teenage years growing up in the projects, it became a competition between teenaged boys to conquer women, and as many as you could. I later realized this is a completely ridiculous way of thinking. However, growing up in the projects wasn't as bad as some would think. We had lots of fun as children playing and just hanging around each other. We had no idea of what poor meant because it's what we lived, and some of us had no idea what being rich meant, only what we saw on television. We played neighborhood games like freeze tag, hide and seek, football, etc. One of my favorite games was house, mommy and daddy and their 20 kids. What's funny is I remember when we played house, abuse was part of the game, fighting is what mommy and daddy would do, or the kids got a whooping. After mommy and daddy would fight they had make up humps. Somehow domestic violence seemed acceptable back in the late 70's and early 80's. I remember hearing the older guys talking about how they would smack their girlfriends in the mouth if they got out of line. I even witnessed one of my big homies beat his girl with his fists just for sassing him right in the middle of the playground while everyone stood around and watched. No one came to her rescue, and it was like I was being taught that it was okay to put your hands on a woman. I even remember my mother telling me stories of how my father put his hands on her, and she didn't sound hurt or victimized when she talked about it, she almost seemed like she wore it as a badge of honor.

Having sex in the projects at a young age is also prevalent. Having many sex partners is not hard to do either. I was 16 the first time I had sex, and that was much later than some. A couple of my friends were fathers at younger ages than that. I remember my first time being with a girl who was 12 years old, and I remember her telling me that I needed more experience. I couldn't believe a 12 year old was telling me this. So I decided to take her advice and I got more experience with her best friend. She had no idea we were having lots of sex behind her back. We were being very irresponsible by having unprotected sex, and she was having sex with one of my friends, being just as reckless. There was no talk about the birds and the bees because we were already living it. By this time my mother and father were heavy addicts. My mother being addicted to alcohol and marijuana, and my dad being strung out on heroin really bad, so they weren't available to talk to me about such things. There was a lot of suppressed pain building up inside of me. The girl who was my first sexual experience got word of my spreading myself around with her bestie and confronted me, and I looked at it as an opportunity to do what I saw my big homie do to his girlfriend on the playground. I did not strike her, but I choked her, and in my mind this was not violence. She became submissive and we went on to have sex soon after that. In my twisted mind I felt this was my reward for checking her about what I did wrong with her friend.

This way of thinking followed me through my adulthood. As the years passed by I continued to womanize, and hold in a lot of pain from my parent's abuse and lack of attention. I did not make it a habit to strike women, I guess I suppressed that too, but later on in my adulthood it would rear its ugly head. Also in the black community seeking mental health services was an extreme taboo. You were considered crazy if you needed therapy. When I was in high school I saw posters about ala-non, and I thought really? I wasn't the one who had the alcohol and drug problem so what the hell was that for? How wrong I was, I truly needed a program like that in my life. However, from the age of 16 to 29 I went through life unguided and reckless. If you remember me saying my mother and grandmother were a tag team when it came to raising me, what I didn't mention is this only lasted until I was 12. My mother decided to adopt two children who are brother and sister. It was my mother's intention to only adopt a girl, but she did not want to split these two beautiful black children up. My grandmother did not agree with her decision knowing that my mother had a drug and alcohol problems. When everything was finalized their relationship became very tumultuous and resulted in a very bad argument. This argument left me without the one who was giving me morals and guidance. So from the age of 15 until I was 18 I did not see my grandmother. I remember going to see her when I was a senior in high school and she had become very frail and sick. I sat with her for hours, and I told her I had been accepted into college and she was extremely proud of me because I was the first person in my family to be accepted into college. Little did I know this would be the last time I would see her, she passed a week later. I was devastated, and I shut down, I almost didn't make it through my senior year. I wound up having to start college on academic probation. When I left for college I started out very ambitious and optimistic. Once I got there I wasn't the most popular guy in school anymore, and I actually became very self-conscious and a little sheltered. All of my untreated issues surfaced and I turned to drugs and alcohol to treat my lack of confidence and this soon turned into a real problem. I got so bad that I did not return after the first semester. I was satisfied with not going back to college, my parents never urged me to return and finish, nor did they question why I didn't return. I got a job, and had my first and second child by the age of 20 and I thought my life was set. I didn't feel the need to use drugs and alcohol anymore, because it became something I actually despised, because of what it was doing to my parents. I thought I was doing well and on my way to overcoming my past, but I still hadn't received any therapy for my issues. From the age of 20 to 29 years old I was living

pretty good, at least I thought I was.

Chapter 6: Kacey and I

Kacey and I met in the fall/winter of 1998. I had started a new job working for a temporary agency. I was told this job was basically to monitor young\ teenage children who were either, displaced, handicapped, or delinquent. I would only have to be what I thought to be a "glorified babysitter", how wrong I was. I was already working a full time job on third shift, at a furniture warehouse and it was only five minutes away from my new job where I got a first shift position. I would leave the warehouse and go to this treatment facility, where it took a few days to adjust. This facility had several cottages that housed the children. Some of the cottages were locked for the higher risk kids, and some were open entry. Being a temp I floated, which meant I wasn't guaranteed to be in the same cottage day to day. Kacey was part of a response team so she would float depending on who needed her. If a cottage was short staffed or a child was having a behavioral problems, Kacey and her co-workers would be called to assist with calming the crisis. I met Kacey a couple of times but only in passing. My first assignment was in a shelter care facility for young offenders who were awaiting court for their offenses. One of the first things I noticed, was that there were a lot of women who worked there. My antennas raised high when I saw this because, I fancied myself somewhat of a playboy. So my first encounter was not with Kacey, plus at the time she was off limits, because the supervisor was her current or ex-lover, at the time I wasn't sure which. He made sure I knew this, because he sensed that I was positioning myself to become the alpha male.

So I decided to pursue another young lady who worked there full time. I began to date this woman who I found out quickly was still involved with her child's father. No big deal, there were plenty of fish in the sea so to speak. Kacey started coming around the cottage more, so of course we conversed more and more. I knew this was "Supe's piece" so I respected the game so to speak, until she opened up to me that her situation with him was complicated. By complicated, that meant he was married. Now all bets were off because he was foul, so now was the chance to challenge him and claim my position as the alpha male, and "I won", enough said. Our first date or encounter was a great dinner and awesome conversation. She was intelligent and funny, and very open about her life, past and present. This made me that much more attracted to her, so after a couple of weeks of conversing on the phone and at work, we knew we were headed in each other's direction. She invited me to her parent's home to watch a movie with her. While watching the movie she opened up about an abusive relationship that she was involved in while attending college in Atlanta. What she told me was almost unbelievable. I could see the pain and even fear in her eyes as she told me of her horrific encounter with this insane dude. I consoled and comforted her. This was the day before she was leaving to visit Atlanta, and this instantly worried me. What if this dude wanted to finish her off for putting him in jail? I told her I didn't want her to go, but she assured me that she would be safe. I knew from this point that she would be my woman and future wife.

Kacey and I began our relationship on February 12, 1999. She was the kind of girl my mother, and grandmother always wanted me to be with, but I wanted to be with many. Instead of me being truthful with myself I went into this relationship with a lie, a lie to be faithful and honest. She was a great girl, the kind of girl I want right now, but right now is 17 years later. I knew of her past indiscretions, but it did not matter to me, who was I to judge because I was an adulterer and fornicator myself. The crazy part of our whole relationship is that we shared a lot of laughs, but also tears to match. We were both basket cases so to speak. We both had issues we needed to deal with before venturing into this union, but we jumped in anyway.

It started out like any typical relationship does with what they call the honeymoon period, but I would soon turn it into a drama filled soap opera. I asked Kacey what made her want to be with a man like me, her response was that she saw potential in me to be a good man. At first I took this as a compliment, but after thinking it over, coupled with my low self-esteem, I took it as me not being good enough for her. It was at that moment I felt like I wanted her self-esteem to be as low as mine, so I made it my mission to accomplish this by any means necessary. Remember I stated earlier if you keep their self-esteem low they won't leave you. So two weeks into the relationship I cheated. I had never had a real relationship before so I tried to sabotage it before my feelings would get hurt. I went to her and revealed my infidelity. She was hurt and she cried, but she stayed. I couldn't believe this, I felt like I got away with murder. At the time I was working two full time jobs and I was sleep deprived. I didn't sleep much so the mixture of no sleep and other women pleading for my affection made me the worse boyfriend ever, but she still stayed. I had never met a woman so tolerant of my B.S., and it made me think that I loved her more but respected her less.

The more we spent time together, the more I knew she was a good woman and I was a piece of shit. So I decided I was going to give her my all, and I convinced her to get her own place so that we could be together more. The place was perfect, it was in a predominately white neighborhood and far from the cities we lived in prior to this, and this meant privacy at its best. I remember hearing the couple upstairs fighting all the time. We would listen to make sure nothing got out of hand, funny how the tables would turn and we soon became that couple. I continued my unfaithful ways around our workplace, but most of the women there were unreceptive to my advances because they knew of my situation with Kacey. The drama didn't begin until Kacey went out with a co-worker and she revealed to

Kacey what I was attempting right under her nose. Kacey confronted me and I became defensive and not only was I defensive I became verbally aggressive and a bully. I couldn't talk my way out of this one so I threw my weight around and it seemed to work. Knowing what she had been through with the guy in Atlanta who verbally and physically abused her, I knew what she would tolerate and accept. I would leave the apartment from time to time, and would go stay at my mother's, attempting to make Kacey think I didn't need her, but after a period of time I would go back to her.

My unfaithfulness became more prevalent, and then "she" happened, I will call her "Aliyah". I remember her first advance towards me. One day Aliyah and I were at work supervising one of the kids who was having some behavioral problems. We were upstairs with this kid until he finally got tired of acting out and fell asleep. While we were sitting in the hallway monitoring all the kids while they were sleeping, things took a turn I didn't expect. She was sitting on a desk with one leg propped on the desk and the other one on the chair. She was wearing a skirt without any panties on, showing me her lady part. She invited me to touch it and so my dumb ass obliged. Afterward I found an excuse to argue with Kacey so I could go back to my mother's house, because Aliyah lived right across the street. I proceeded to get to know her lady part personally, plus learn a few more pornographic tricks. I soon went back home to Kacey to try to stay in this unhealthy union, but she had another agenda. She began to insight Kacey by singing songs around her that represented infidelity, "If your girl only knew". She would even sing the song when she saw Kacey and me together. The I-team reporter/co-worker who had already been giving Kacey information, told her about me and Aliyah. At this point Kacey and I are engaged, and World War 3 began. Since I had been able to have my way with how I treated Kacey, I turned our battles up a notch by becoming more verbally aggressive by bullying and threatening her. I did not hit her, but the threats and bullying were just as bad, and I was able to get away with it because at this point I don't think Kacey would have been able to be without me. These types of confrontations became more prevalent as time went on in our relationship, and I had no idea some of these confrontations were being provoked by Kacey. I mentioned earlier how sleep deprived I was, and I believe that contributed to my extreme frustration. So I decided to take some anger management classes, because I no longer wanted to be abusive towards her. After about five sessions, I felt I was magically cured, no more abuse.

Being with her made me realize I was at a point in my life when I should be enjoying the fruits of my labor, hell we were both making some good money, but I had responsibilities taking care of my mother and two daughters. I was not only paying my mother's bills but I was also supporting her addiction. Kacey took care of us financially so I could take care of my other household. But as I stated I was in desperate need of a break, so I planned a trip for the two of us to go to Florida. We needed to get away from the everyday turmoil between her and I. I-77 to I-95 here we come. The ride down was really nice, we talked, laughed, and even discussed how to repair our relationship, so things seemed perfect for a short period of time. We planned to get a hotel room, but my cousin and his wife extended their home to us, so we stayed with them. The first thought that came to my mind was "out of town sex!!!!!!" We had a pretty good sex life. Kacey was really all I needed in a woman physically, although she didn't think so. The reason she didn't think so was because I told her she was inadequate in the bedroom and that she needed to be more freaky. I said that as a ploy to get her to be open to a few things in the bed, but all in all she satisfied me, really I was just trying to get out of trouble when I got caught cheating. When we got there Kacey wasn't comfortable with us having sex in someone else's home. I didn't give a rat's ass if we were in the White House, I wanted what I wanted. Now remember I was an alpha male, I got what I wanted when I wanted it, so I thought. She was adamant at first, but after being verbally abusive to her, she let her guard down. Not because I was so charming and loving, but because she was fearful of what I would do to her. We had some form of sex, and I just remember being an asshole about it by making her feel as if she wasn't enough for me.

The trip went really well for me, but not for her. The whole time we were there I rode her about what she was wearing. Kacey was not a fashionista by any sorts, she wore sweats and Sketchers, and I donned named brand, the expensive stuff. I remember her telling me if we lived by my standards we would be the best looking broke couple in the country. I did tend to be a tad frivolous with money and she was EXTREMELY frugal. So what she wore wasn't important to her. Kacey and I started a joint bank account just for this trip and we were supposed to put an equal amount away each week, and because she was more disciplined than me, she wound up saving much more money than I did. One day before we went to Disney World I took it upon myself to go out and pick an outfit that I wanted her to wear. I tried to make it look like it was a present, but she was not having it, because she felt as if I were trying to control her. The same day I bought her the outfit, I bought a woman back home that I liked a present as well. The whole trip to Florida was miserable for her and I was so caught up in myself I didn't even notice it. Disney World was our next stop, and when we got there I took it upon myself to offer to pay for my cousins to get into the parks. I didn't consult with Kacey, but didn't think I needed to since they were letting us stay with them, but I should have discussed it with her first. From the time we got there until the time we left I was on the phone off and on with the girl back home. Now this was the girl I mentioned earlier who was still involved with her kid's father. Kacey seemed a little suspicious, but I blew it off like I was talking to my mother or some friend. Our trip had come to an end and it was time to drive home. I was content because the trip was a success in my eyes. I had grossly overspent money that I partly contributed to, and I was a complete jerk pretty much the whole trip. I don't remember why we got into it, but I do remember it getting physical. I snatched her from the back of the head and spoke very harshly to her. After I calmed down we drove home. A man should never touch a woman in any way or harm her. A man who does this is a coward. Yes I am calling myself a coward.

Things went back to normal when we got home, my infidelity and abusive ways seemed to turn up a notch, the more I got away with the more abusive I became. After I got away with so much I had developed a sense of entitlement, I felt untouchable. I could do all the wrong I wanted and I would be forgiven. All I had to do was be on "sex punishment" until she felt like forgiving me. It was cool because I was still getting sex outside of our relationship. As soon as the shoe was on the other foot I couldn't handle it. After months of my infidelity, Kacey admitted to me that she had gone out with one of our co-workers and even shared a kiss with him. I became FURIOUS!!!!!! And so ENRAGED!!!!!!! All I could think of was to destroy something or someone, that someone would be the closest person to me at the time, so it was her. I hit and screamed and I hit and screamed some more, then I grabbed every gun that I owned, and laid them on the bed. I had two nickel plated 9mm handguns, one 22 automatic which I had bought for her, but she didn't want any part of owning a gun, and then there was "My Bitch" a 12 gauge pistol grip Mossberg pump shotgun. I pointed each one of those guns at her that day, I wouldn't allow her to leave, go to the bathroom, or answer the phone. Only God saved me and her that day. She eventually talked me down, and made me realize that my actions had led her to this point of cheating on me. I then became severely depressed and I told her I was going to kill myself, and she became frantic. I took the 9mm, cocked it and put it to my head, walked in the bathroom and locked the door behind me I heard her crying and pleading with me not to kill myself. This was the first and only time I truly contemplated suicide. After about 20min of hearing her pleading and calming me down, I came out. She held me for a long time and we both cried ourselves to sleep.

This wasn't our last instance of physical aggression. There was another instance where we had gotten into an argument that turned violent. We were arguing and I decided to sleep in our guest bedroom because I was extremely tired from working three straight shifts. Kacey refused to stop bickering, so I went into the guest room and closed the door. She fussed through the door and when I stopped responding to her she flung the door open and threw an object at me, hitting me directly in my right eye. After being temporarily blinded, I leaped out of bed and pounced right on top of her. Up until this point I had never hit Kacey with a closed fist. I punched her directly in the eye she had hit me in. She screamed and cried while I continued to slap and shake her, but she managed to get to the phone and call my father. At this point I was punching holes in the walls, and she handed me the phone to talk to my father. He began to scream and yell at me, and I calmed down and so did he. He told me of how he had become abusive at times with my mother and how the cycle of abuse had been passed down to me. Even then I was still in denial. I wasn't an abuser. I could stop at any time. I was so wrong. Throughout the relationship little incidents would turn into major catastophes, and Kacey would even start a fight from time to time. I remember calling home once to ask her if she wanted something to eat and she said she had already eaten, so I stopped and got myself something. Upon arriving home I sat down to eat some chicken, and I could tell Kacey was on edge about something. She never had a problem letting me know when there was a problem, and she began bickering and cursing at me. She told me that I was a slob because a crumb of chicken fell on the floor. I told her as soon as I was done eating I would clean up after myself. This brought no relief to her and she continued on with her rant until I became very loud and aggressive. At this point she became very submissive and obedient. For whatever the reason this behavior turned me on, the more I yelled, the more she would become like my property. She would even ball up in the fetal position on the bed and brace herself to prepare for being hit, it's like she expected every situation to turn into a fight.

The more this happened the more physically aggressive I would become, it was almost like foreplay, because almost every time after I was physically aggressive we would have make up sex. I can remember a few times when she didn't respond in a submissive manner and I would get more aggressive just because I wanted that side of her to come out. Power and control became my motivation for my behavior. When I was younger I suffered from very low self-esteem and an identity complex, so my verbal and physical aggression towards Kacey made up for all of my instability, at least I thought so.

"My day of shame"

Shame is a painful, social emotion that can be seen as resulting "from comparison of the self's action with the self's standards. [1] but which may equally stem from comparison of the self's state of being with the ideal social context's standard. Thus, shame may stem from volitional action or simply self-regard; no action by the shamed being is required simply existing is enough. Both the comparison and standards are enabled by socialization. Though usually considered an emotion, shame may also variously be considered an affect, cognition, state, or condition."

Finding yourself is probably one of the hardest journeys you take in life. I still don't know completely who I am. I am a business owner, and a single father of two, and I find myself still searching, but a little closer to knowing who I am. I have made many mistakes in my life, but on June 9, 2000 I made the biggest mistake, and it would change my life forever. I assaulted and threatened the life of the woman I was supposed to love and marry. It was an out of body experience, a day we will both never forget.

The day began with us attending training at work. While in the training, Kacey and I were called back to aid staff with some of the kids who had been acting out. When we arrived to the cottage several children were displaying behavioral problems. We were asked to assist with a regular knuckle head kid. We were considered strong staff so this is why we were asked to aid with this particular kid. Immediately the child had to be physically restrained. While on the floor, this kid kicked, screamed, spit, and hit. We were in a door way so the first thing I noticed was Kacey and who I called "BIG HEAD", but she called him "Safety", flirting with one another. The second thing that set me ablaze was the fact that the door we were by was ordered to be closed, so the other children would not be incited by this kid's loud screaming. My hand happened to be in the crack of the door, I was bracing myself so I wouldn't put all of my weight on this child. When the door was closed my hand was smashed, and I screamed louder than the kid was screaming. The strange thing about it the kid thought it was funny, because of the laughter it de-escalated his behavior, but escalated my already building anger. Not only was I in tremendous pain, now I could only hear giggling and horseplay between Kacey and Big Head. All I could think about was shutting up all of the laughter they were doing, and I figured my 9mm would change all of the "high jinx" carrying on. After the kid was taken to his room I asked Kacey to speak with me so I could question her about this clown. Since I was on her shit list due to all of my antics and my high jinx, she refused to talk to me. This made my notion to get that nickel plated lie detector even stronger. The shift would be over soon, and I figured I would convince her to talk to me, but I needed to get my insurance policy so to speak just in case she refused again. I couldn't wait, I was so anxious, so I ran out to my car to get my piece. I then asked again to speak with her, she declined once again. We were standing in the doorway of this house where "BIG HEAD" was, and I flashed her my business so she knew I meant business. All rationale for me was retired for the night and I lost it right then and there. In fear she ran upstairs, so I cocked it to load, and I ran right behind her so she couldn't tell anyone. She was afraid and I knew it because this wasn't the first time I pulled out a gun on her, so I knew fear in her when I saw it. Since she didn't want me to hurt her or anyone in the cottage she agreed to talk to me. I convinced her to get in my car, and I asked and asked her to tell me the truth about her and "BIG HEAD". She told me they were only friends and I did not believe her. I knew this woman very well because of our lengthy relationship and I felt I knew her body language very well. I didn't believe her so I threatened to go find him and put a bullet in him if she didn't tell me the truth.

I felt my soul sliding out of my body, and a pure evil force entering it. I took off with us in the car down this winding road exiting the facility where we worked. I know I was doing 80mph and I screamed, yelled, and threatened until she admitted that there was more to her and this huge headed fag. I thought she was done with him after she stepped out on me with him before. For some reason I calmed down enough to take her back to the facility, but I wasn't all the way calm, because now I was on the hunt for him. A close friend of mine who worked with us happened to be standing outside when we arrived back at the job. Kacey immediately pleaded with him to help her, and calm me down, and this he accomplished. The only thing I remember after that point was going home to my mother's. I couldn't sleep because whatever entered my body was still there. I stayed up all night trying to call her, trying to think of a way to convince her to take me back. After all the chaos I just put her through, I had some nerve, but I was playing on the fact that I felt she was naïve and gullible. She would not answer my phone calls, so I drove an hour to what used to be our place and I sat outside for hours. I even stalked around the window to see if I could hear her talking to someone. I sat in my car for hours because I knew what time she would be leaving to go to work in the morning, because I felt like I could get her to take me back.

Eventually she came out, and I walked up on her aggressively and demanded that she hear me out. Out of true fear she screamed for help and reached for her cell phone. I grabbed it and slammed it to the ground, grabbed her arm and showed her the gun again, but this time she was determined to fight for herself. An old woman had come outside, Kacey screamed for her to help, the lady ignored her, but this was enough to distract me. Kacey ran to her car and jumped in, started it and pulled off. I also jumped in my car and gave chase. As I stated, we lived in a predominately white community, and I was so surprised no one called the police. The police station was only 5 minutes away, but Kacey sped past the station which I found very strange. She went right back to where I originally started all of this mess, the work sight. She ran into the main cottage and locked the door behind her. At this time I got out yelling for her to come out and speak to me, but no reply. At this point whatever I felt enter my body the night before, did its job and left me right then and there, leaving me numb. By now I figured the police had been called so I waited for them because I was tired and I knew I had gone too far. I was hurting because the woman I loved was gone, and I had hurt her to the point of no return. I knew prison was inevitable because I grew up around enough crime and violence to know that there was no coming back from this. My life would be changed forever, and I was truly ashamed of myself and I knew I had failed her, my parents, and myself. The next step would be one only a man could take, and to some degree I was still a boy. After a few days in a city jail, made bail, and I was a wreck. I knew my fate but I still wanted Kacey and for her to help me. I saw her sad eyes in court so I figured I still had a chance and I was right. After obeying the restraining order for about a week, I reached out to her. We reconnected, but I was in no shape to be with this woman, and she didn't need to be with an abuser like me, with untreated issues. It eventually came crumbling down swiftly because I started displaying the same abusive tendencies as before. This would be it, after another verbal blow up, she had enough and I was a goner.

Even after this I still attempted to contact her by going out to her place. I knew she had a thing for puppies so I found a smelly stray puppy and tried to convince her to take me back, no dice. The final attempt was to go the spiritual route. You would have thought I was straight from the Middle East. I dressed up in my finest Muslim garb. I had my holy book in hand, knocked on the door. She answered but did not let me in. She called the police this time, and this would be the last time I would see her until I had to go back to court. I will never forget that day. I was sitting in this small cell waiting for them to come get me for over an hour, I sat in this cold metal room with no one but guilt and shame. When they finally came for me, I was led down a corridor into a court room. The worst feeling came over me because there were two ladies that only had my best interest at heart. They were sitting there looking extremely sad because of my silliness and horrible decision making. The looks on their faces are etched into my psyche for life. On my left was Kacey, on my right was my mother, and I felt like crap. I had already been told that I was offered a plea deal of two years, so I knew my fate. I was turned around to face this mean ass female judge, who all my life I felt was under me, because she was a female, and now this female had my life in her hands. She spoke to me in a way that no woman had ever spoken to me in my life. I kept this poisonous way of thinking up until this point, and all I could think to myself was if I was her husband I would be beating the crap out of her, with her hot mouth. Then she said it!!!!!!!!!!!!!! She said if I attempt to contact, harass or bother Kacey again she would put a 0 after that 2 and give me 20 years. Afterward I was allowed to face these completely hurt women. I turned to my mother, with tears in my eyes and my heart skipped many beats, and my voice was cracking as I apologized for her having to endure such a disgraceful event. Then I apologized to Kacey, but I was still trying to make her look like she was at fault for what I had done. I told the judge that she had taken me back, and that she participated in me breaking the restraining order that was against me. Kacey yelled out, "no I didn't", and the judge yelled my sentence, and had me quickly escorted out of her court room.

Chapter 7: Forgiveness

After being released from prison, I worked hard not to become a negative statistic. I rebuilt my life brick by brick, and I busted my tail to get my life back on track and live up to my true potential. When my mother passed away, I knew it was my calling to open a restaurant. Watching her bust her tail in other people's establishments, I was inspired to do this and I did. My partners and I were building a brand. There was one thing that was unsettled in my life, and that was to heal from what caused my incarceration. I always wanted to bring closure to me and Kacey's situation. I always daydreamed about how our interaction would be, but I knew it probably would never happen, so I prayed about it and left it alone. The restaurant had been open about four or five years, and out of nowhere I heard my name being called while I was in the back room of the kitchen. My partner told me I had company, and I never thought in a million years it would be Kacey. I walked up front and in total awe, there she was. The woman who I treated worse than anybody who ever crossed my path was standing there with the warmest smile. I walked around the counter where we embraced each other. With a lump in my throat the first words from my mouth was "I'm sorry", and to my surprise she returned with the same. At this time I felt God's spirit move through me, the same way I felt that evil spirit move through me that night I hurt her. God's spirit brought joy and redemption, and I knew this could not be easy for her. We sat and talked for a while and I could sense her uneasiness. It was a little weird for me, because I had dreamt about this for so long, and I didn't want to mess it up by saying anything wrong, so I wanted everything right to come out. I didn't want to blow the only chance to make things right between us. I asked her if she thought we could ever be friends after this and she replied no. As disheartening as this was I fully understood. I felt like this was it, I would never get to laugh or talk with the woman who I truly loved once before, for the second time. I was still very thankful for the opportunity to make what I did wrong fade away. When she left I knew I would never see her again unless it was in passing. I felt there was still something that wasn't fulfilled with our interaction, and I felt we had more to do. I have heard that faith without works is dead, and I felt we had work to do, but how could I convince her to work with me.

I continued to reach out to her subtly without being overbearing or a stalker, so I patiently waited for the opportunity to present my plan to her. Finally after a million tries, she was willing to communicate with me on social media. I knew there was a chance for us to change the world. I always knew she was going to be great and change lives, even though she might not have recognized it. Together we would be great, but only time would tell. True forgiveness is hard, it's so easy to hate, but it strips you of so many blessings. After a while of saying hello here and there, I would send her messages making small talk just to let her know she was on my mind. I knew she was preparing to write a book. I always knew she wanted to help women in crisis, so I figured it would be some kind of self-help book. Little did I know it was an autobiography, self-help book, and then it happened! The book was released and I kind of knew that I was featured, but I didn't know how much. It took me a while to muster up the courage to buy it, and once I did, it took me a while to read it. When I did I was reminded of everything that she told me about her relationships before me. Then the moment of truth came and I was given the name "Muslim". Then I read and read, unable to put the book down for even a second. A flurry of emotion went through me, anger, sadness, and confusion, I was a mess. At first I felt like she embellished a lot, but then it all started coming back to me. I almost forgot it was about me, and wanted to find this dude and beat his ass, but then I remembered this dude was me, what a bitter pill to swallow. I prayed at that moment, and I knew God had forgiven me because of the life I was now being blessed with, but I realized I had not forgiven myself completely. Remember I said I felt that me and Kacey's journey was not over, well I remembered that I had ideas about me and Kacey going around speaking to men and women. One big hurdle, how do I convince her to go along with me in doing this? I reached out and asked her how she felt about maybe speaking publicly and co-authoring a book. The book would be about our experience with domestic violence, but she was reluctant and said she would pray about it. Still respecting her wish to keep our distance somewhat, I left her alone. After some time went by, I received a message stating that God had answered her and she felt it was the right thing to do. It has been almost a year later, and we have brought up some ugly incidents, and even some great ones. Even though we weren't completely healed, since we interacted and related with one another, the healing is now almost complete.

It is my duty as a man to reach out and help whoever I can. It is my sincere hope that this message reaches the masses and can help a man, woman, or child who may be experiencing some form of abuse. Please know that it doesn't have to go too far, and please get help before it does. It seems almost every time I watch the news or a television program there is some form of violence happening. I know that I can't reach everybody, but if I just reach one, and they can reach another, and that cycle of breaking the cycle continues, then we can live in a better society.

Conclusion

Lying in your bunk at night is probably the worst part of prison because all you got are your thoughts. Most of them were about her, did she really love me? Did she miss me? Was she even thinking about me? Or was I just out of the picture? I loved her, but I didn't love God first nor did I love myself. If you are not whole, you can only give someone part of yourself. If you're not together spiritually or in touch with who you are, it's impossible to give yourself to anyone or anything. I would reflect back on our situations that became violent, and I would begin to question "what made me get so angry, and why couldn't I control it? I remembered when it got to the point of rage, I had no control, and it cost me. Counselors tell you to recognize your triggers, and one of the things you're supposed to do is remove yourself from the situation. What happens when she won't allow you to leave, or she gets in your pathway to the door? It is very important to at least acknowledge that you have a problem. Once you can admit that you need help, GO GET IT!!!   I have never gotten into statistics or numbers when it came to domestic violence, I just knew that it was a lot of men and women out there who needed help or to be pointed in the right direction. I also know that you can't help someone who doesn't want or realize they need help. It is my only intention to enlighten and teach. I am tired of seeing women get hurt or even die at the hands of someone who is out of control. During my time in prison I came up with the idea to reach out, but I had never seen or heard of a couple who had experienced domestic abuse, and reach out together. How would I pull this off? Kacey wanted nothing to do with me, and neither did her loved ones, and I understood why.

After being released and becoming a productive citizen, I sort of lost my drive to do this. I wasn't going to reach out to Kacey because I was living my life and she was living hers. Over the years I had gotten married and inherited a wonderful stepson and in laws, plus we had two beautiful children together. I was doing alright, but I continued to hear news about women being hurt and even murdered. I knew something needed to be done. Even with the distraction of having a family and new responsibilities, I still felt I had unfinished business. I still needed to reach out. God was telling me that my journey wasn't complete. I went through more anger management, which this time was great because I had an awesome instructor. So after finishing, the thought of reaching out hit me even harder. I wanted even more to reach the people who needed the same help and guidance I once needed. If I had the opportunity to reach each and every man who is going through the same thing I did, I would tell them just to be honest with yourself, get in touch with yourself mentally and spiritually, and GET HELP IMMEDIATELY!!! To every woman, I would say have zero tolerance for any kind of abuse. Once he gets away with one form of abuse, it's only going to escalate to another form of abuse, and get worse. If you are in the middle of a situation already GET HELP, and GET OUT!!!! If I can reach anyone with this book, I hope it gives you enough strength and courage to get your life on track, and to also reach out to someone else who may be experiencing the same issues, you have gone through. Each one, teach one.